English - Bengali

1000 SIGHT WORDS MADE EASY

energy
শক্তি

Have you used solar energy?

didn't
না

I didn't know.

over
উপর

He jumped over it.

copy
কপি

Is the copy machine working?

map
মানচিত্র

Did you look at the map?

next
পরবর্তী

Take the next step.

let
দিন

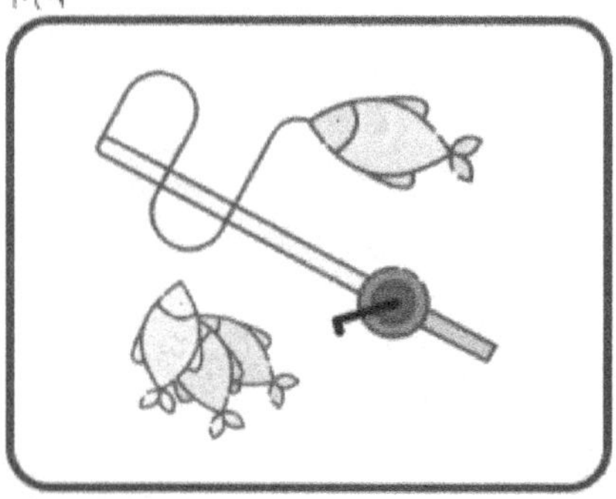

Will you let me go fishing?

spread
ছড়িয়ে পড়া

Spread your wings.

body
শরীর

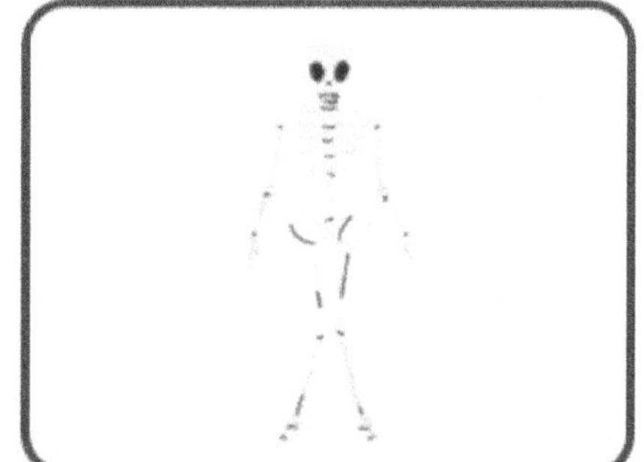

The body has a lot of bones.

trouble
কষ্ট

Did you have car trouble?

exciting
উত্তেজনাপূর্ণ

This is so exciting!

mile
মাইল

It's a mile from here.

sand
বালি

They played in the sand.

suppose
অনুমান করা

I suppose we could go to the pool.

fun
মজা

They had fun at the beach

winter
শীতকালীন

Winter is here!

save
সংরক্ষণ

Try to save some money.

contain
ধারণ করা

What stories does it contain?

follow
অনুসরণ করা

Follow the teacher.

ten
দশ

Did you hit all ten pins?

himself
নিজে

He smiled to himself.

earth
পৃথিবী

Our planet is Earth.

fast
দ্রুত

A cheetah is fast.

see
দেখা

He can't see without glasses.

oh
উহু

Oh! It's a puppy!

difference
পার্থক্য

What's the difference?

do
করা

Do you like pizza?

enough
যথেষ্ট

Did you eat enough pancakes?

single
একক

A single balloon

early
দ্রুত

She had to get up early.

so
সুতরাং

We had so much fun.

day
দিন

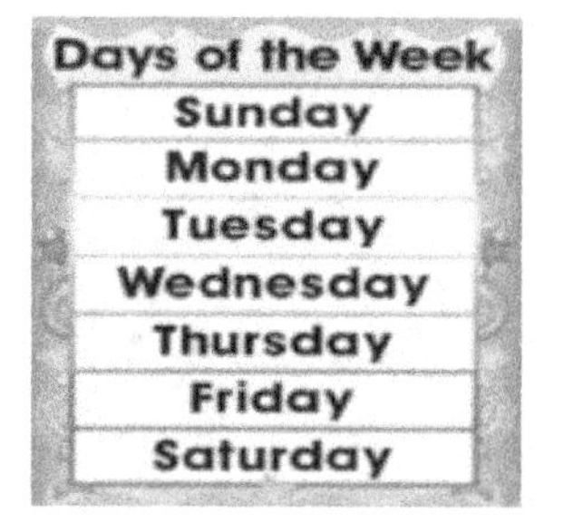

What day is it today?

doesn't
না

Doesn't it sound beautiful?

me
আমাকে

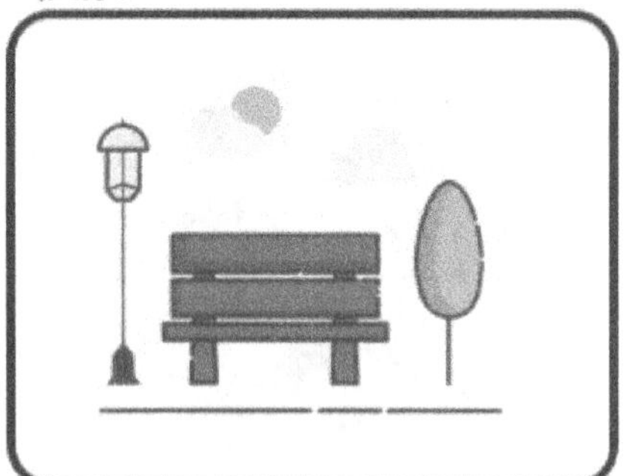

Come with me to the park.

box
বক্স

What's in the box?

wide
প্রশস্ত

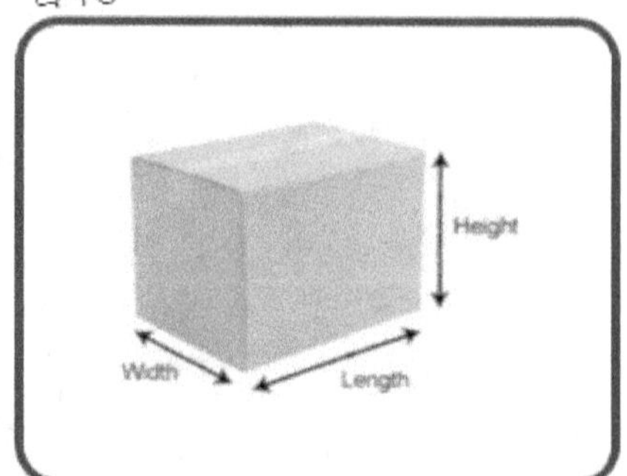

How wide is the box?

rock
শিলা

A diamond is part of a rock.

figure
ব্যক্তিত্ব

Who was able to figure it out?

wild
বন্য

What is your favorite wild animal?

explain
ব্যাখ্যা করা

Please explain it again.

until
পর্যন্ত

I work until 5 o'clock.

received
গৃহীত

She received an award.

lie
মিথ্যা

It's never good to lie.

time
সময়

What time is it?

team
টীম

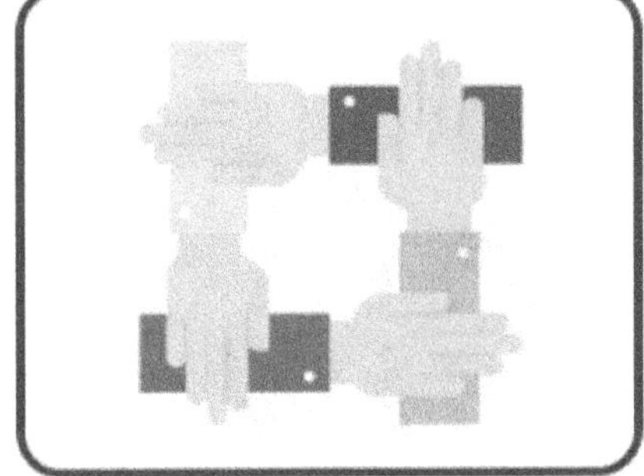

Are you on the basketball team?

song
গান

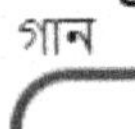

We will sing a song.

rain
বৃষ্টি

It started to rain.

study
অধ্যয়ন

It's time to study.

insects
পোকামাকড়

Do you like insects?

value
মান

The value of family is greater.

girl
মেয়ে

The girl wore pink shoes.

easy
সহজ

He thought it was easy.

care
যত্ন

She'll care for him.

art
শিল্প

Do you like to look at art?

small
ছোট

The ladybug is small.

march
প্যারেড

Are you going to march with the band?

subject
বিষয়

What is your favorite subject?

bank
ব্যাংক

I need to go to the bank.

hundred
শত

She made a one hundred on the quiz.

state
অবস্থা

Which state do you live in?

free
বিনামূল্যে

They set the tiger free.

on
চালু

Please turn on the light.

most
সবচেয়ে

Most students like to help.

all
সব

It's all gone!

wear
পরিধান

Did you find a suit to wear?

bad
খারাপ

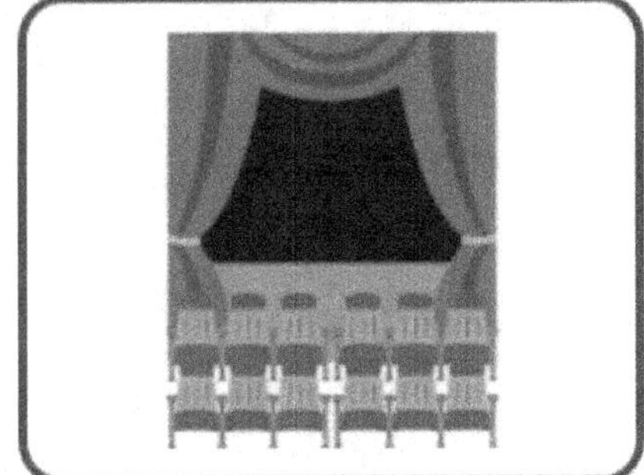

The movie was bad.

place
জায়গা

This is my favorite place.

he
তিনি

he waved hello.

minutes
মিনিট

How many minutes left?

brought
আনীত

Everyone brought a present.

already
ইতিমধ্যে

I already bought groceries.

round
বৃত্তাকার

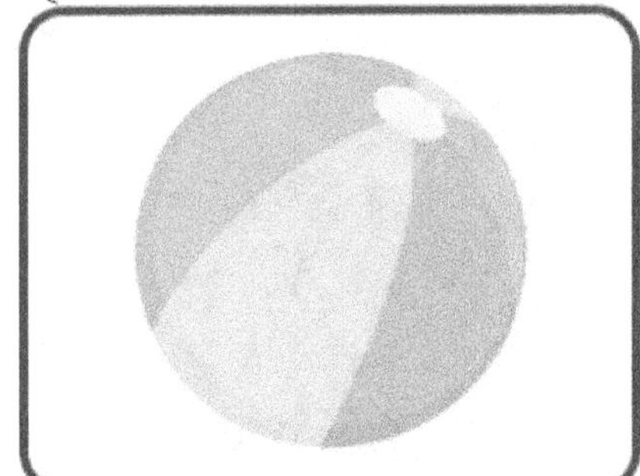

The soccer ball is round.

boy ছেলে	**were** ছিল	**flight** ফ্লাইট
		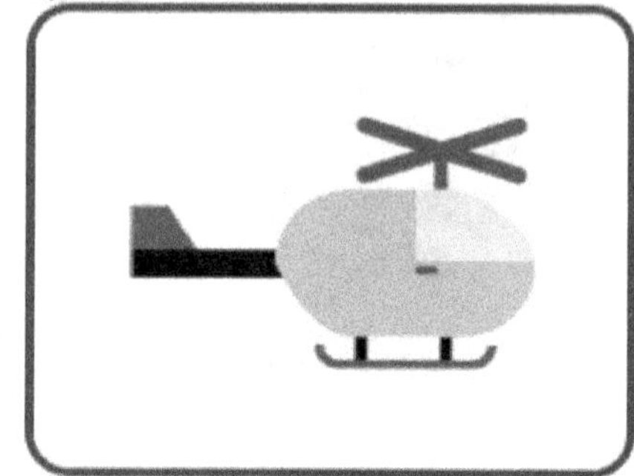
The boy played a basketball.	We were at the carnival.	The helicopter took flight.
seat আসন	**front** সদর	**passed** গৃহীত

The girls took a seat in the sand.	She was at the front of the line.	She passed her driver's exam.
though যদিও	**watch** ঘড়ি	**since** থেকে

Even though she's busy, she read alot.	Do you wear a watch?	Since you like cookies, let's make some.
great মহান	**read** পড়া	**divided** বিভক্ত
		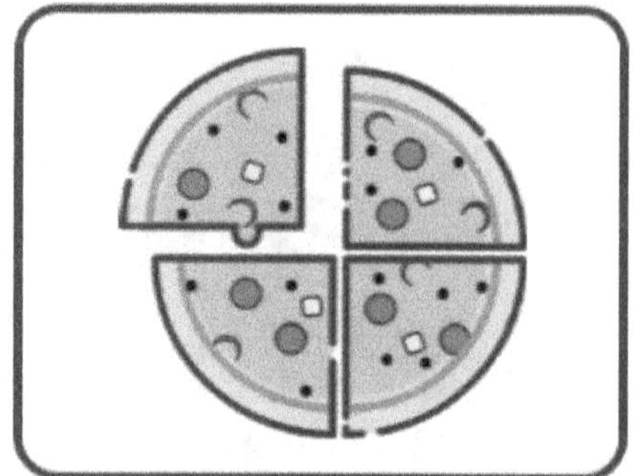
Great job!	Do you like to read?	It was divided up.

nation
জাতি

Which nation are you from?

company
প্রতিষ্ঠান

What company do you work for?

them
তাহাদিগকে

I invited them to my party.

together
একসঙ্গে

They went shopping together.

french
ফরাসি

She's a French bull dog.

saw
করাত

We saw a UFO.

factors
কারণের

What are the factors of these numbers?

what
কি

What is your question?

ran
দৌড়ে

They ran the race.

a
একটি

A girl sang.

electric
বৈদ্যুতিক

Do you own an electric car?

break
বিরতি

Time for a break.

covered
আবৃত

Snow covered the car.

hours
ঘন্টার

How many hours is it open?

low
কম

My battery is low.

father
পিতা

Her father walked her to school.

indian
ভারতীয়

It's an Indian elephant.

finally
পরিশেষে

She finally smiled.

turn
চালু

Turn in your homework.

page
পৃষ্ঠা

Please turn the page.

understand
বোঝা

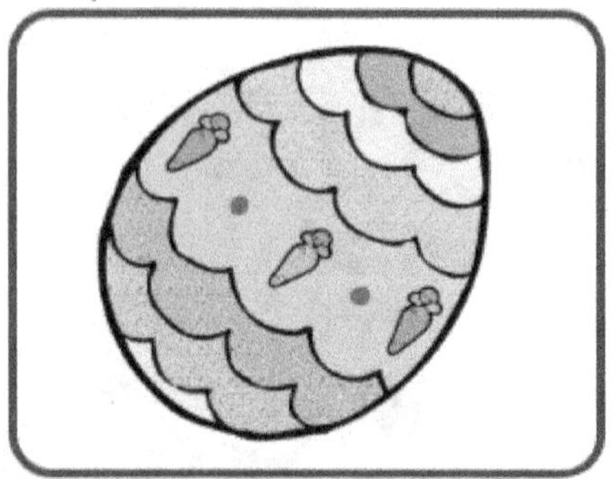

Do you understand the homework?

hunting
শিকার

We're hunting for Easting eggs.

sugar
চিনি

Sugar cube for your tea?

decided
সিদ্ধান্ত নিয়েছে

We decided to go to the lake.

old
পুরাতন

Those are old toys.

top
শীর্ষ

We put a cherry on top.

rule
নিয়ম

Which rule did you break?

these
এইগুলো

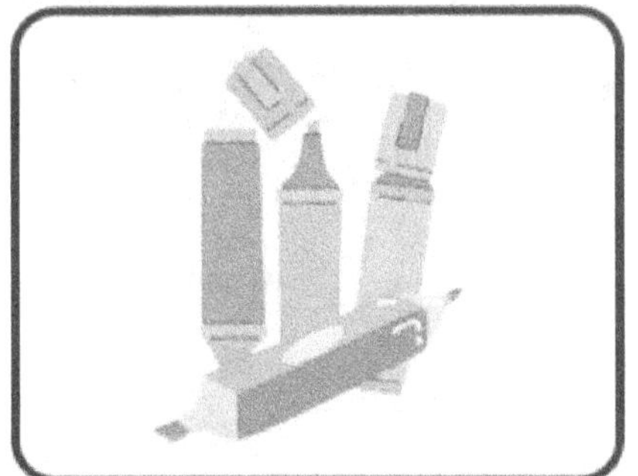

These are my markers.

suffix
প্রত্যয়

What is the suffix of the word?

being
হচ্ছে

She is being shy.

corn
ভুট্টা

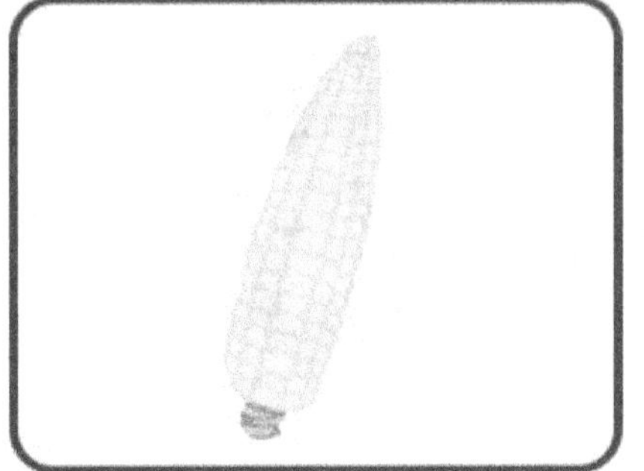

Do you like corn?

lifted
উত্তোলিত

The jeep is lifted.

amount
পরিমাণ

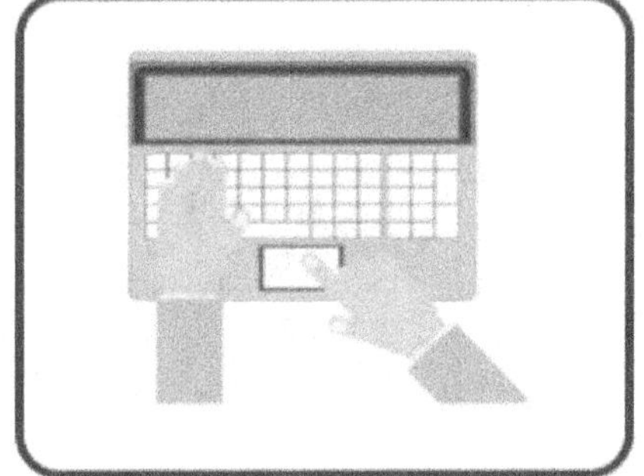

What amount of work do you have left?

elements
উপাদান

Look at the periodic table of elements.

near
কাছাকাছি

We are near the beach.

spell
বানান করা

Please spell the word.

tell
বলা

She wanted to tell a secret.

division
বিভাগ

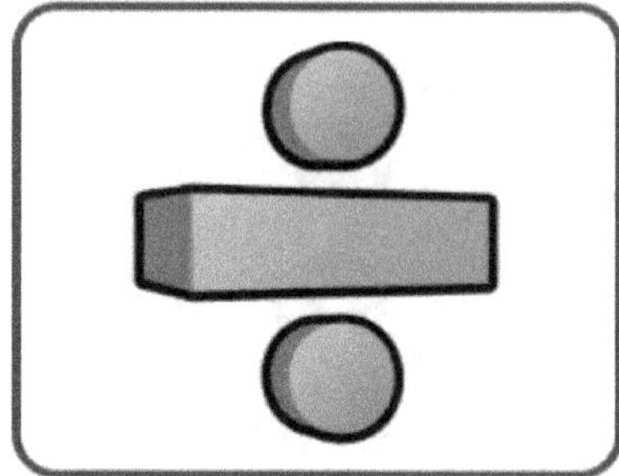

We did division today.

modern
আধুনিক

She loves modern art.

crowd
ভিড়

There was a large crowd.

change
পরিবর্তন

I save my change.

kind
দয়াশীল হওয়া

Be kind to each other.

the
দ্য

The weather is nice.

could
পারা

Could you see the moon?

our
আমাদের

She was our teacher.

begin
শুরু করা

You may begin your exam.

certain
নির্দিষ্ট

Certain words are harder than others.

different
বিভিন্ন

They use different balls.

group
গ্রুপ

They were working in a group.

located
অবস্থিত

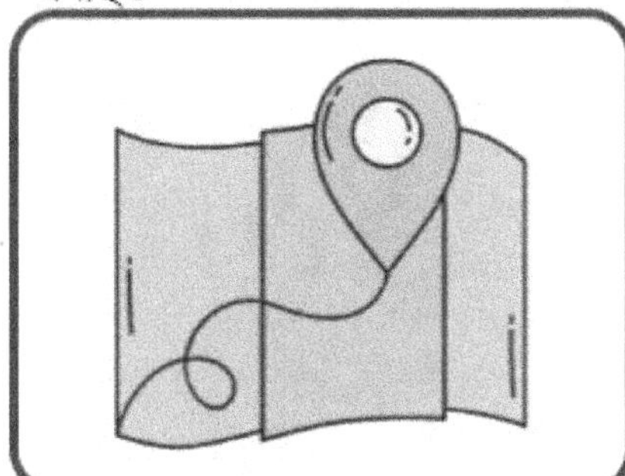

Where is the store located?

although
যদিও

Although sunny, it's cold out.

soft
নরম

The teddy bear is so soft.

there
সেখানে

It's over there.

main
প্রধান

There's the main gate.

president
সভাপতি

Make sure you vote for president

burning
জ্বলন্ত

The candles were burning.

pushed
ধাক্কা

She pushed the stroller.

south
দক্ষিণ

Mexico is south of the US.

substances
পদার্থ

What are these substances?

still
এখনো

I still want ice skates.

go
যাওয়া

May we go to recess?

strange
অদ্ভুত

That's strange looking.

second
দ্বিতীয়

She won second place.

details
বিস্তারিত

Look for the details.

loud
অট্ট

The concert is loud.

cried
cried

She cried.

fly
মাছি

Did you fly there?

years
বছর

You are five years old today.

string
দাড়ি

It's a red string.

men
পুরুষদের

The men played football.

actually
প্রকৃতপক্ষে

I actually like strawberry.

consonant
ব্যঞ্জনবর্ণ

What is the consonant?

sigh
দীর্ঘশ্বাস

Did you sigh?

cotton
কার্পাস

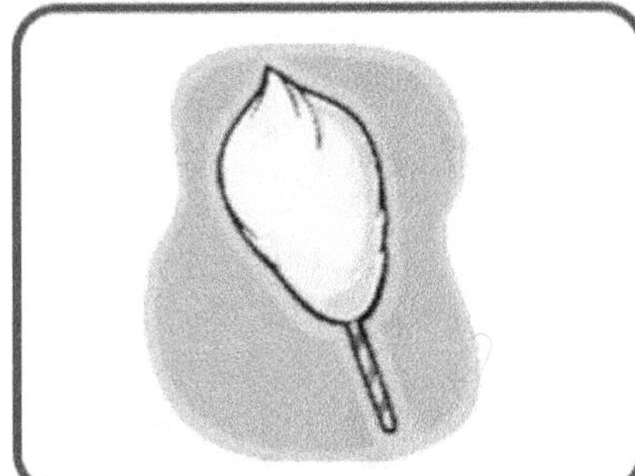

A q-tip is made of cotton.

difficult
কঠিন

I found this difficult.

kept
রাখা

She kept hold of the balloon.

race
জাতি

The race is about to begin.

must
অবশ্যই

You must raise your hand.

black
কালো

He has a black cat.

vowel
স্বরবর্ণ

What are vowels?

example
উদাহরণ

This is an example of a bird.

touch
স্পর্শ

The cheerleader can touch her toes

write
লেখার

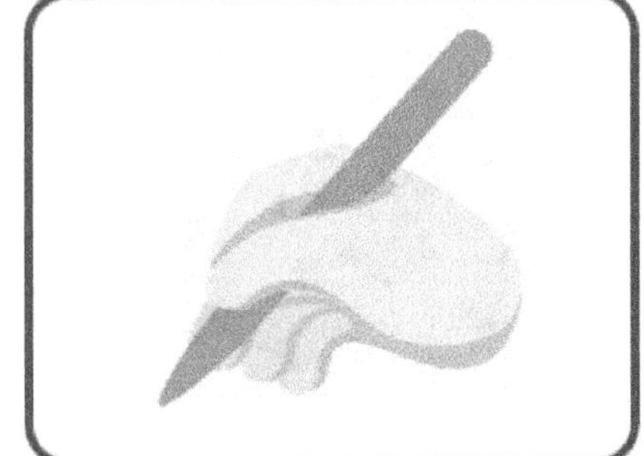

Please write your name.

numeral
সংখ্যা

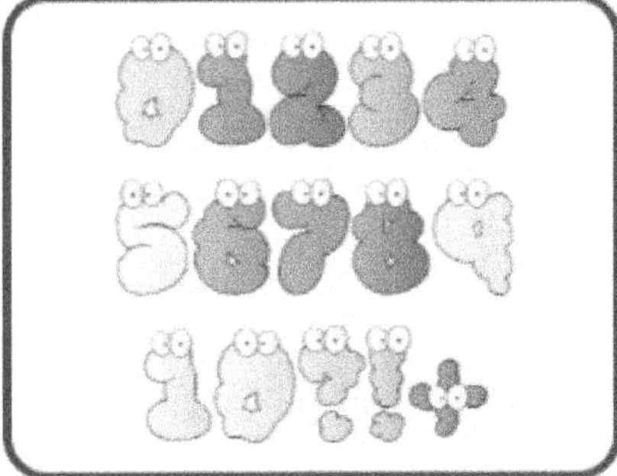

Which numeral did you choose?

crops
ফসল

How are the crops growing?

dry
শুষ্ক

Try to stay dry.

plural
বহুবচন

What is the plural of a mouse?

heat
তাপ

Please heat up the oven.

boat
নৌকা

Did you want to go on the boat?

deal
লেনদেন

Did you agree on the deal?

mark
ছাপ

I used a check mark.

they
তারা

They were jump roping.

instead
পরিবর্তে

Do you drink tea instead of coffee?

put
করা

Please put the supplies away.

various
বিভিন্ন

I watch various shows.

glass
কাচ

Did you clean the glass?

lake
হ্রদ

We're still going to the lake.

face
মুখ

They were at the face painting booth.

took
গ্রহণ

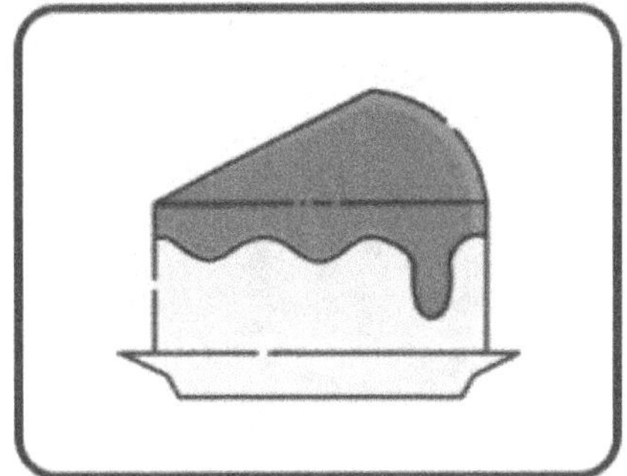

He took the last piece.

wire
টেলিগ্রাম

This telephone has a wire.

same
একই

Did you get the same answer?

better
উত্তম

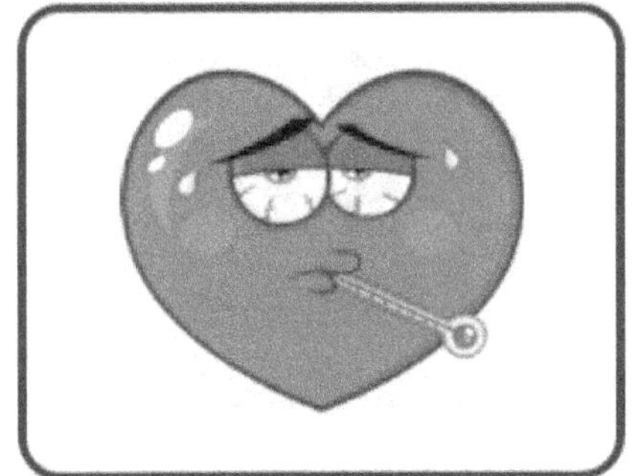

Feel better soon!

far
এ পর্যন্ত

How far is it?

ready
প্রস্তুত

Is it ready?

snow
তুষার

Let's play in the snow!

bear
ভালুক

He loves his old teddy bear.

period
কাল

You put a period at the end.

heard
শুনেছি

I heard you like music.

movement
আন্দোলন

Movement is important.

something
কিছু

Did you hear something?

been
হয়েছে

I've been to Mexico.

especially
বিশেষত

She especially liked writing.

fear
ভয়

I have a huge fear of clowns.

i
আমি

I like icecream.

king
রাজা

Have you ever met a king?

broken
ভাঙ্গা

Her heart is broken.

probably
সম্ভবত

It's probably on the list.

rich
সমৃদ্ধ

I want to be rich.

class
শ্রেণী

It's a class party.

suggested
প্রস্তাবিত

I suggested you do your homework.

religion
ধর্ম

What religion is it?

him
তাকে

John sat next to him.

drive
ড্রাইভ

Does your dad drive you?

up
আপ

We walked up the stairs.

prepared
প্রস্তুত

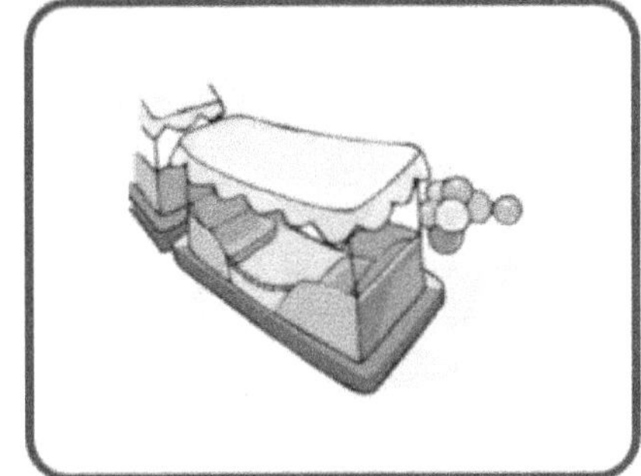

She prepared for the exam.

park
পার্ক

Let's go to the park.

their
তাদের

They liked their teacher.

might
হতে পারে

It might rain today.

cold
ঠান্ডা

It's cold outside.

happy
খুশি

Music made him happy.

rest
শিথিল করা

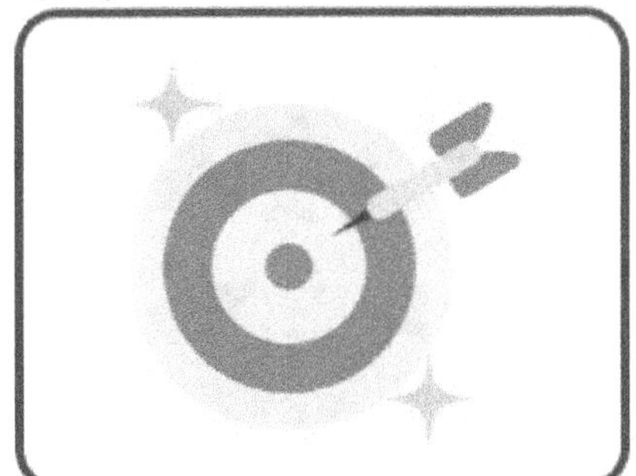

You needed to rest.

center
কেন্দ্র

The bullseye is the center.

captain
অর্ধিনায়ক

Who is the ship's captain?

brown
বাদামী

It's a brown cow.

one
এক

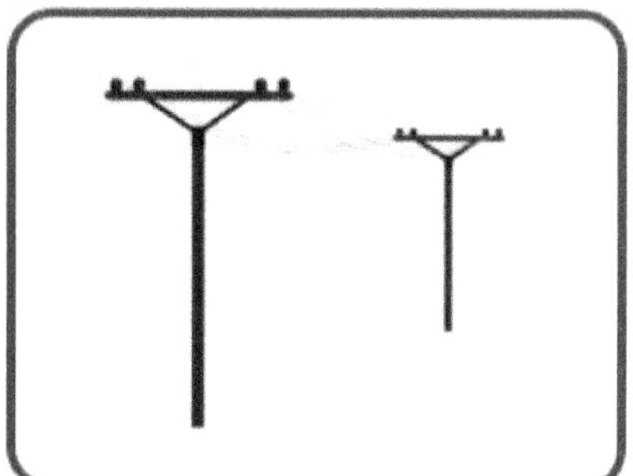

There is one cupcake left.

pole
মেরু

Is that a telephone pole?

wheels
কায়দা করে

Did you buy new wheels?

temperature
তাপমাত্রা

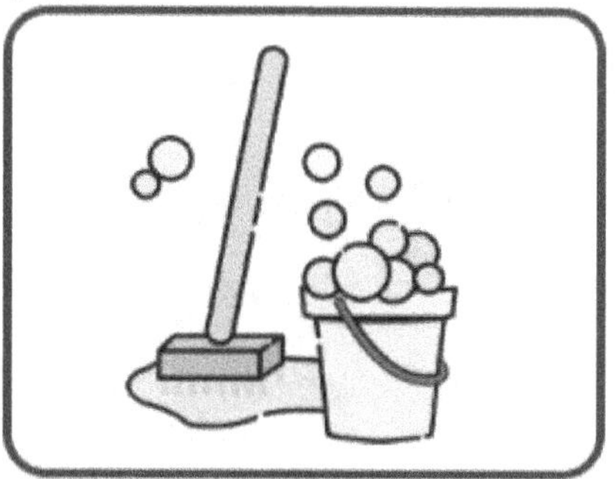

What's the temperature?

floor
মেঝে

Did you mop the floor?

much
অনেক

How much is the camera?

three
তিন

It's the number three.

end
শেষ

She watched to the end.

means
মানে

She got her by means of a taxi.

field
ক্ষেত্র

It's the new football field.

heavy
ভারী

It's really heavy.

wind
বায়ু

The wind is too strong.

underline
নিম্নরেখা

Underline the word.

fit
হইয়া

How much did you fit in there?

mountains
পর্বত

There are alot of mountains here.

got
পেয়েছেন

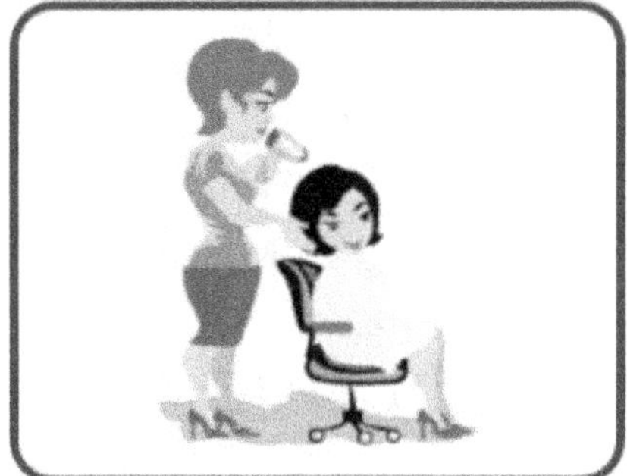

She got a hair cut.

dark
অন্ধকার

It's dark at night.

keep
রাখা

Can you keep a secret?

full
সম্পূর্ণ

The basket was full.

those
সেগুলো

Those are great cookies!

world
বিশ্ব

I want to travel the world.

drop
ঝরা

Did you drop and crack it?

test
পরীক্ষা

How'd you do on the test?

grew
বড় হয়েছি

The flower grew.

iron
লোহা

I need to iron my shirt.

root
মূল

Which team do you root for?

more
অধিক

I need more time.

it's
এটা

It's a tiger cub.

phrase
ফ্রেজ

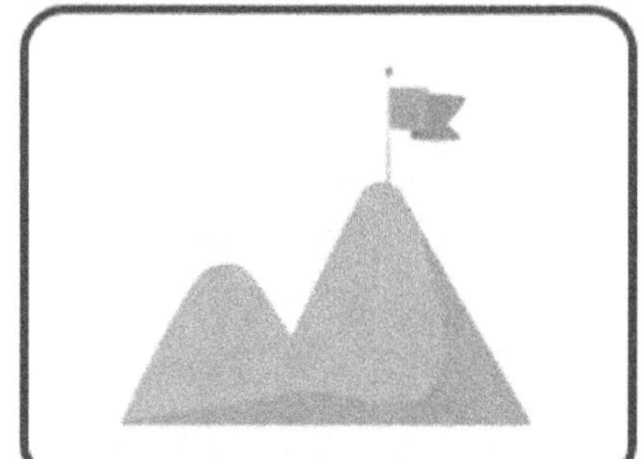

His phrase inlcuded a penny.

beat
বীট

Our team beat yours.

square
বর্গক্ষেত্র

A square has four equal sides.

forest
বন। জংগল

Where is the forest?

into
মধ্যে

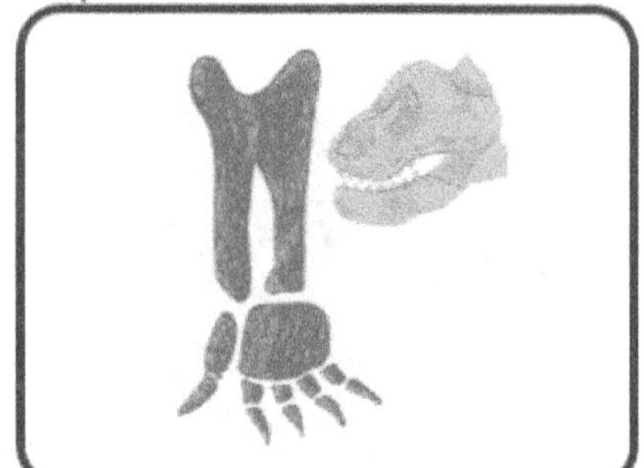

That goes into the bin.

bones
হাড়

Did you see the dinosaur bones?

carefully
সাবধানে

Handle those carefully.

never
না

I've never broken my leg.

fine
জরিমানা

He had to pay a fine.

want
প্রয়োজন

I want to ride my bike.

wash
ধোয়া

We decided to wash the car.

forward
অগ্রবর্তী

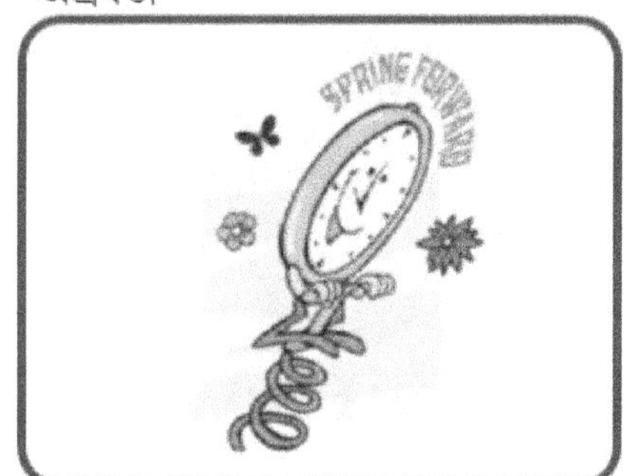

Spring forward the clocks.

mind
মন

Your mind is full of imagination.

dance
নাচতে

They dance like professionals.

act
আইন

Do you like to act in a play?

hard
কাঠিন

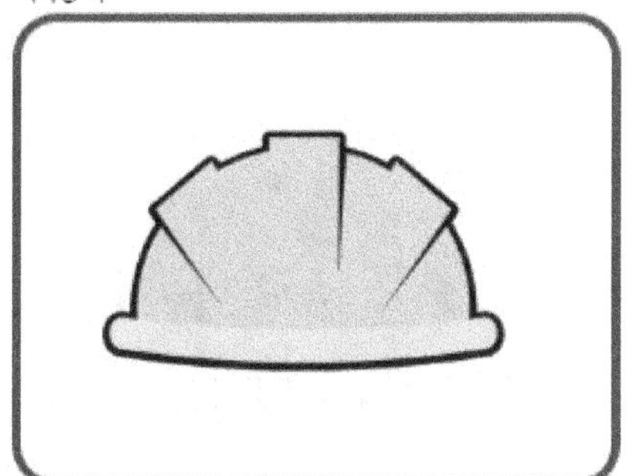

He wore a hard hat.

choose
পছন্দ করা

Which one did you choose?

symbols
প্রতীক

What do those symbols mean?

record
নথি

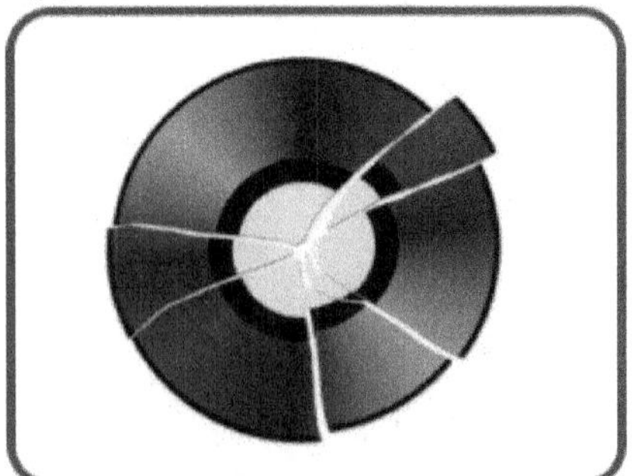

Who broke the record?

soldiers
সৈন্য

They are soldiers.

steel
ইস্পাত

The new building used steel.

members
সদস্যদের

All the members were there.

hope
আশা

Let's hope.

column
স্তম্ভ

Did you read the newspaper column?

as
যেমন

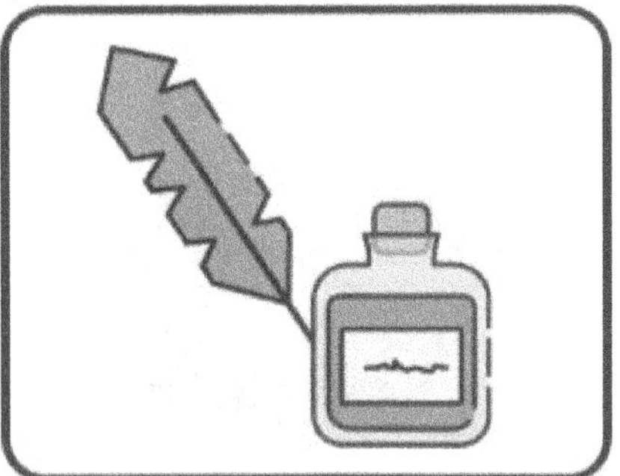

It's light as a feather.

unit
একক

A centimeter is a unit of length.

observe
মান্য করা

Do you want to observe the stars?

she
সে

She had fun with her friends.

once
একদা

Once upon a time…

valley
উপত্যকা

They traveled to the valley.

wife
স্ত্রী

His wife is a teacher.

color
রঙ

What is your favorite color?

win
জয়

Did you win?

after
পরে

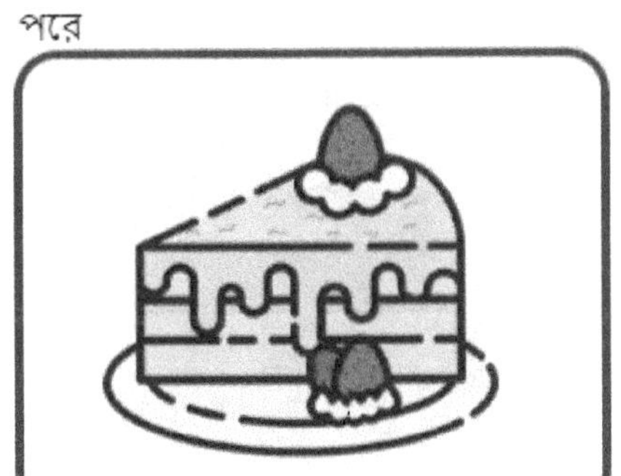

You may have dessert after dinner.

cents
সেন্ট

That's just my two cents.

measure
পরিমাপ করা

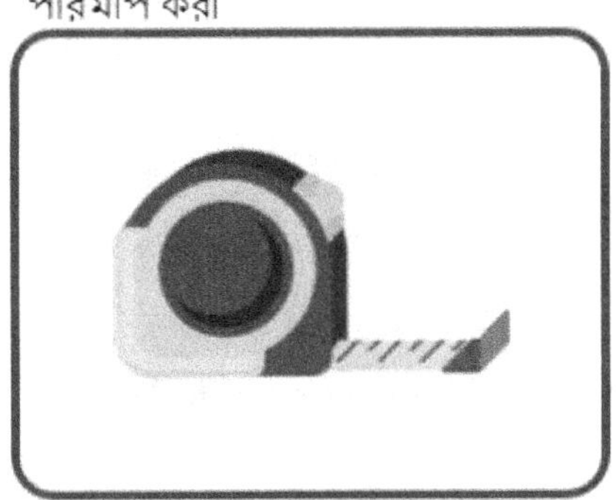

Did you measure it?

student
ছাত্র

The students worked together

fraction
ভগ্নাংশ

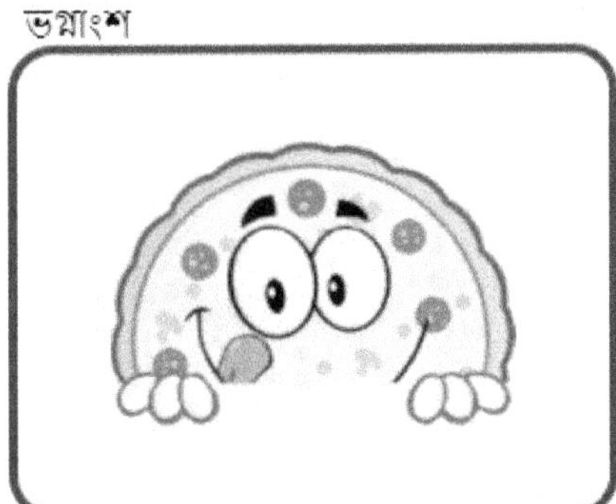

What fraction of the cake did you eat?

party
পার্টি

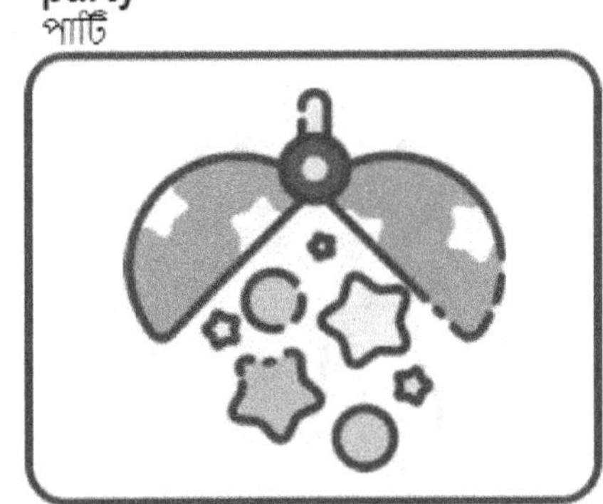

How was the party?

believe
বিশ্বাস করা

I believe in Santa Claus.

trip
যাত্রা

Did you enjoy your road trip?

of
এর

I'm proud of you!

cut
কাটা

You use scissors to cut.

draw
আঁকা

Do you like to draw?

week
সপ্তাহ

This week is busy.

developed
উন্নত

They developed a strong friendship.

fall
পড়া

Be careful to not fall.

board
তক্তা

That's her surf board

possible
সম্ভব

Will it be possible to grill this weekend?

piece
টুকরা

This piece fits.

corner
কোণ

Turn at that corner.

out
আউট

Take the dog out for a walk.

greek
গ্রিক

Have you ever had Greek food?

did
করেছিল

Did you buy popcorn?

usually
সাধারণত

Usually I have coffee.

simple
সহজ

It was a simple dress.

quiet
শান্ত

Quiet in the library.

almost
প্রায়

It's almost lunch time.

told
বলা

I told you I made a snowman.

own
নিজের

Do you own a computer?

became
হয়ে ওঠে

She became a nurse.

fire
আগুন

We made a fire.

size
আয়তন

What's your shoe size?

speed
দ্রুততা

What's the speed limit?

farm
খামার

They have cows on the farm.

hole
গর্ত

Did you get a hole-in-one?

yes
হ্যাঁ

Yes, I want to go.

bell
ঘণ্টা

Ring the bell.

statement
বিবৃতি

He worked on his thesis statement.

would
হায়

Would you like some juice?

meat
মাংস

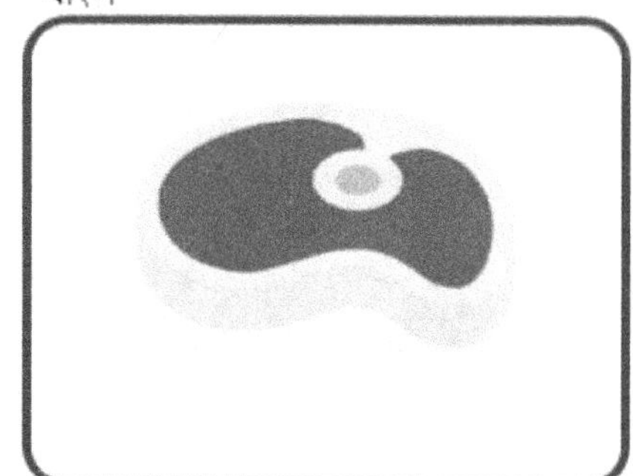

Do you eat meat?

problem
সমস্যা

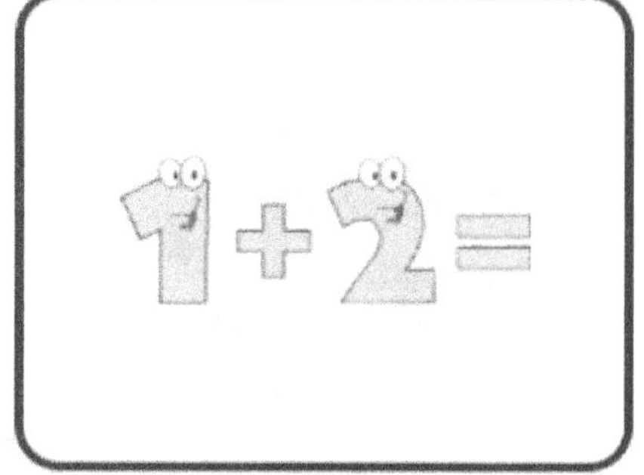

Let's solve the problem.

part
অংশ

He ate part of my homework.

force
বল

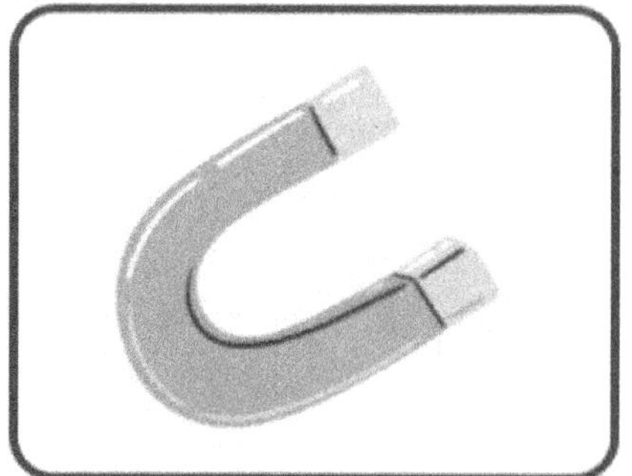

We learned about force.

thick
পুরু

That's a thick book.

home
বাড়ি

Is this your home?

city
শহর

He worked in the city.

addition
সংযোজন

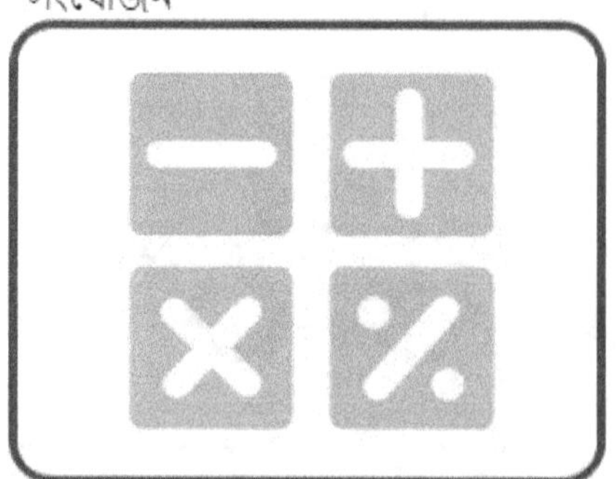

Do you learn addition?

farmers
কৃষকদের

Farmers work hard.

wait
অপেক্ষার

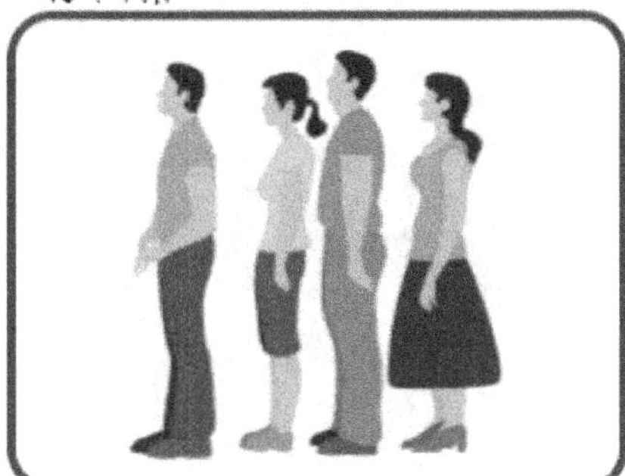

How long did you wait?

hair
চুল

Did you get get your hair cut?

famous
বিখ্যাত

She's a famous actress.

smell
গন্ধ

I love the smell of cookies!

smiled
হেসে

He always smiled

soon
শীঘ্রই

Dinner will be ready soon.

clothes
বস্ত্র

Did you hang your clothes up?

return
প্রত্যাবর্তন

They were excited to return.

sometimes
কখনও কখনও

Sometimes we watch tv.

huge
বিশাল

Those trees are huge!

france
ফ্রান্স

Have you ever been to France?

wings
ডানা

She was flapping her wings.

yet
এখনো

Are we there yet?

filled
ভরা

It's filled with flowers.

molecules
অণু

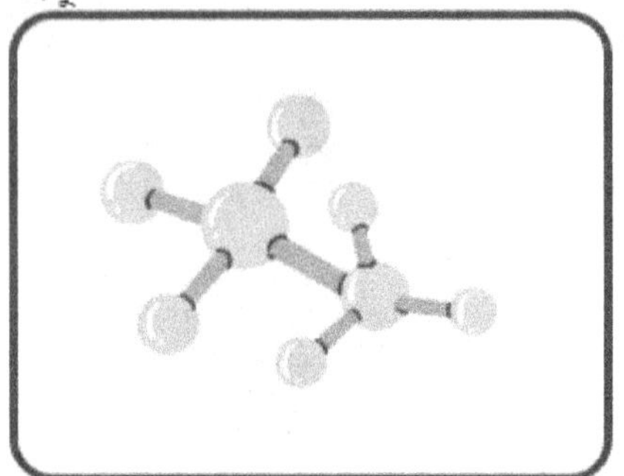

Are those molecules?

toward
দিকে

She taught toward the front.

trade
বাণিজ্য

I'll trade you my sandwich for yours.

friends
বন্ধুদের

They are my friends.

sun
সূর্য

The sun was out.

ever
চিরকাল

Don't ever doubt yourself!

seven
সাত

She has seven lipsticks.

her
তার

It is her doll.

design
নকশা

Did you design this?

tiny
অতি ক্ষুদ্র

It's so tiny.

entered
প্রবিষ্ট

She entered the room.

rather
বরং

I'd rather be reading.

result
ফলাফল

What was the result of the election?

brother
ভাই

Is that your brother?

number
সংখ্যা

Her jersey number is twelve.

terms
পদ

Did you learn new vocabulary terms?

fact
সত্য

Is that a fact or opinion?

remain
থাকা

Please remain in your seat.

light
আলো

The light turned yellow.

life
জীবন

Life is about friends and family.

few
কয়েক

She wanted a few more minutes.

during
সময়

We learn a lot during class.

just
মাত্র

The train just left.

whose
যাহার

Whose guitar is it?

other
অন্যান্য

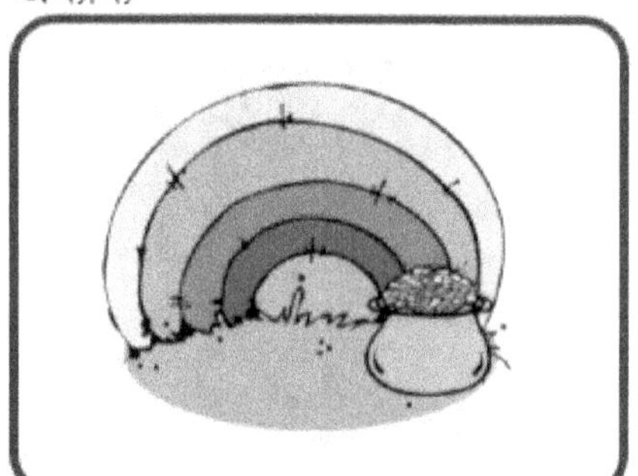

What other colors do we need?

good
ভাল

The hamburger was good.

animal
পশু

My favorite animal is a lion.

british
ব্রিটিশ

Who is the British monarch?

talk
আলাপ

Let's talk.

children
শিশু

Four children sang.

however
যাহোক

He hates milk, however he drank it.

machine
মেশিন

It's grandma's sewing machine.

either
পারেন

Will either of you wash the car?

remember
মনে রাখা

I'll try to remember.

woman
নারী

The woman was on her way to work.

try
চেষ্টা

Try again, please.

or
অথবা

Do you like cats or dogs?

again
আবার

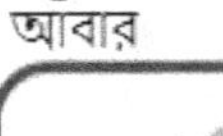

May we go on the ride again?

itself
নিজেই

The house won't clean itself.

tools
সরঞ্জাম

May I borrow your tools?

agreed
একমত

They agreed on music.

less
কম

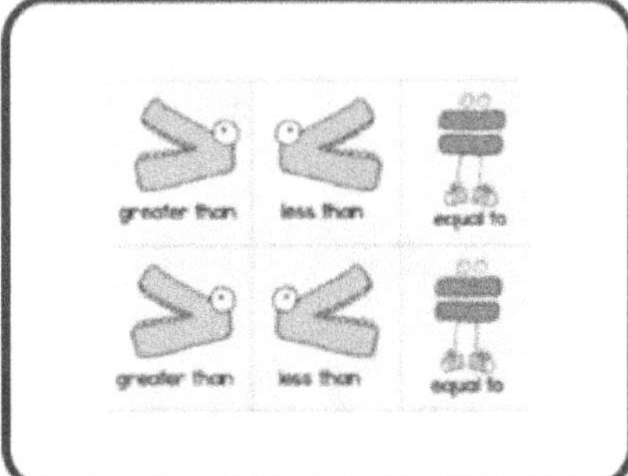

Three is less than five.

think
মনে

Think about it.

than
চেয়ে

He is taller than her.

are
হয়

We are friends.

about
সম্পর্কিত

It's about lunch time.

oxygen
অক্সিজেন

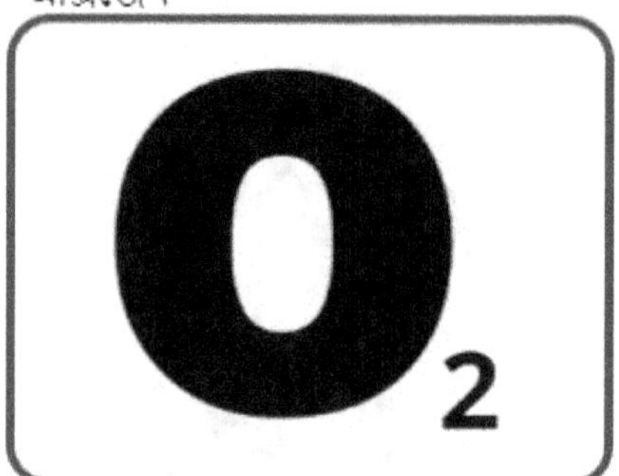

What is the symbol for oxygen?

bottom
পাদ

There's treasure at the bottom.

mall
মুদ্গর

Do you want to go to the mall?

that
যে

That is my house.

business
ব্যবসায়

They opened their business.

compound
যৌগিক

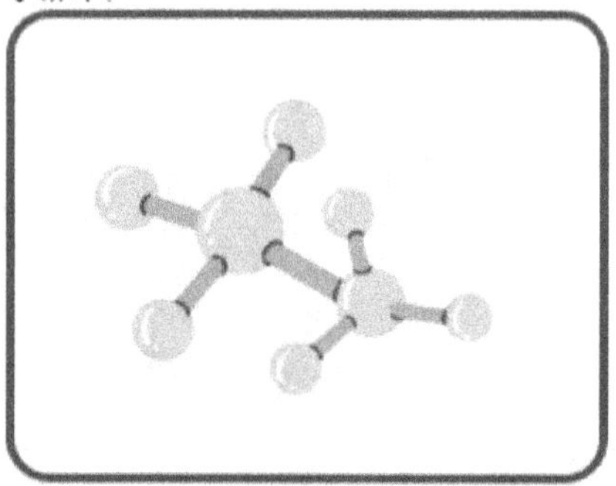

This is a compound.

way
পথ

It's a one way street.

true
সত্য

It's true love.

close
ঘনিষ্ঠ

Please close the door.

safe
নিরাপদ

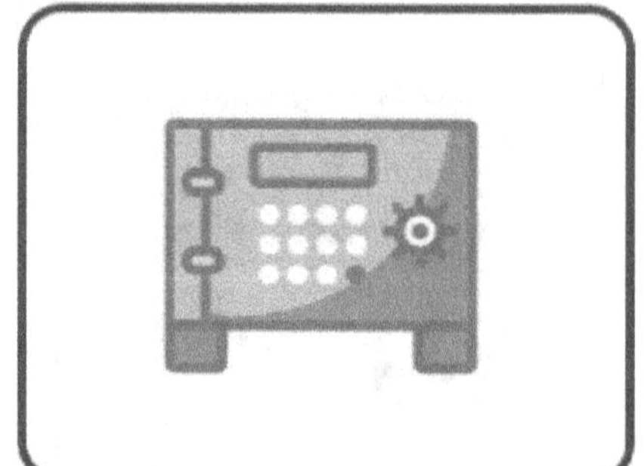

Do you have a safe?

ago
পূর্বে

It happened a long time ago.

special
বিশেষ

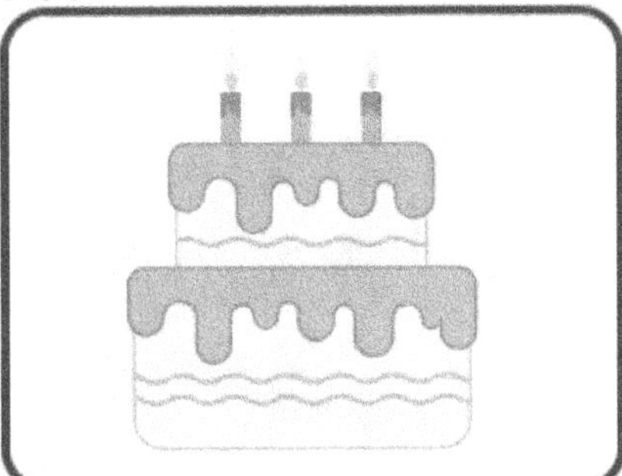

It's a special cake.

also
এছাড়াও

I also like baseball.

bed
বিছানা

We have a bunk bed.

cows
গরু

How many cows does he have?

stream
প্রবাহ

We played at the stream.

nose
নাক

My nose is running.

water
পানি

Drink more water.

garden
বাগান

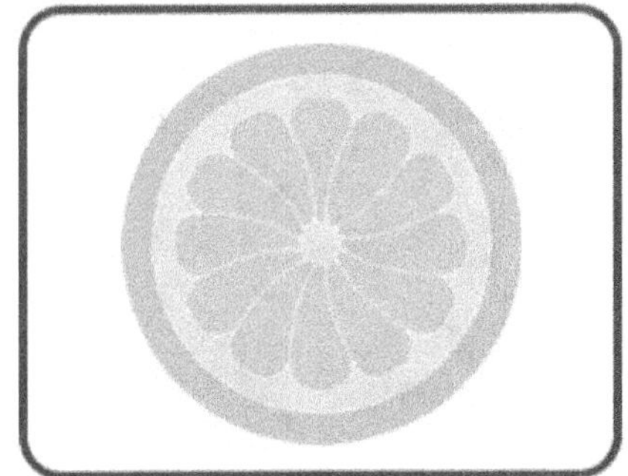

She worked in the garden

half
অর্ধেক

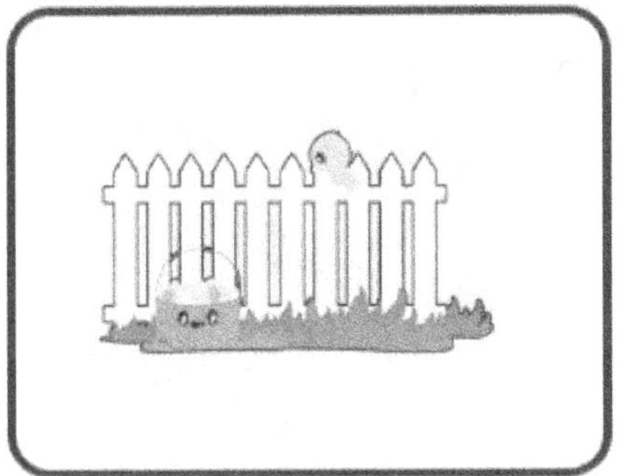

I hate half the orange.

section
অধ্যায়

This section is fenced off

engine
ইঞ্জিন

The fire engine parked there.

whether
কিনা

Whether you go by bus or not, go.

lead
নেতৃত্ব

We were in the lead.

very
খুব

He is a very good singer.

quite
পুরোপুরি

You are quite busy

like
মত

Do you like to read?

we
আমরা

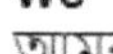

We went to the beach.

blood
রক্ত

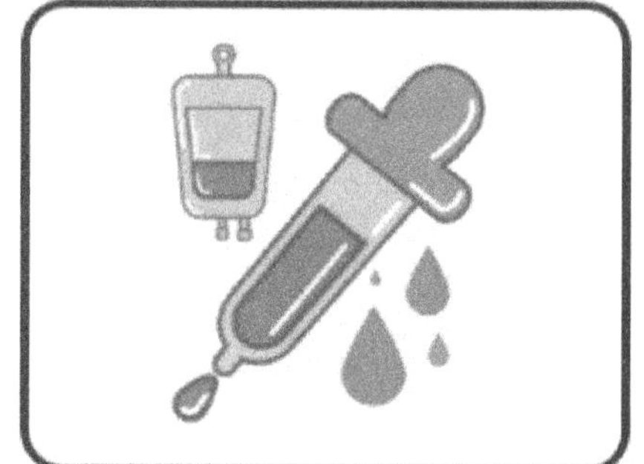

I donated blood.

surprise
আশ্চর্য

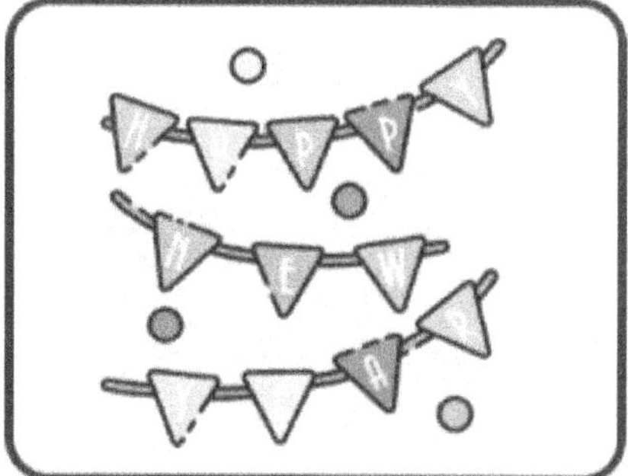

She threw a surprise party.

rose
গোলাপ

Thank you for the rose.

i'll
আমি করব

I'll call.

direct
সরাসরি

Did you direct the film?

air
বায়ু

The air was cold.

off
বন্ধ

The rocket blasted off.

middle
মধ্যম

She stood in the middle.

little
সামান্য

He has a little sister.

determine
নির্ধারণ

Did you determine where to go eat?

poor
দারিদ্র

Did you do poor on the exam?

book
বই

I'm reading this book.

equal
সমান

Does it equal four?

written
লিখিত

It was written down.

base
বেসবল

Do you play first base?

army
সেনা

Is he joining the army?

food
খাদ্য

They made a lot of food.

truck
ট্রাক

Is thaty our truck?

pounds
পাউন্ড

The price was in pounds.

summer
গ্রীষ্ম

Are you ready for summer?

miss
হারানো

You may correct any you miss.

hand
হাত

Please hand in your work.

sharp
তীব্র

Those are sharp scissors.

by
দ্বারা

John sat by Jane.

idea
ধারণা

I have an idea!

seem
মনে

You seem busy.

suddenly
হঠাৎ

It happened suddenly.

am
টা

I am hungry.

america
আমেরিকা

Columbus sailed to America.

store
দোকান

What store did you go to?

building
ভবন

I made a building with legos.

woman
নারী

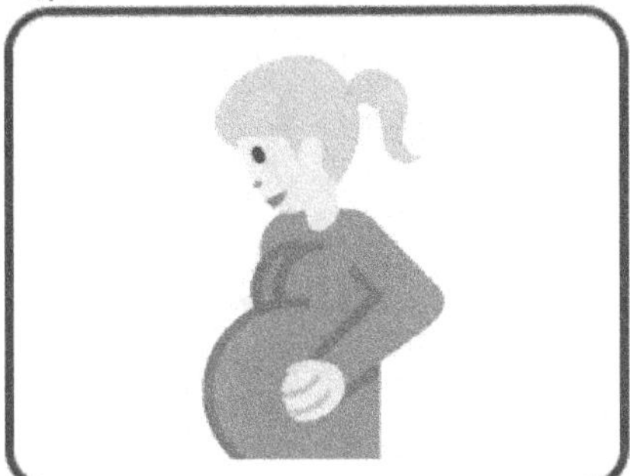

Is the woman pregnant?

sentence
বাক্য

Complete the sentence.

sea
সমুদ্র

The ship is at sea.

show
প্রদর্শনী

Show your work.

before
আগে

Sharpen your pencil before the test.

island
দ্বীপ

The island was beautiful.

interest
স্বার্থ

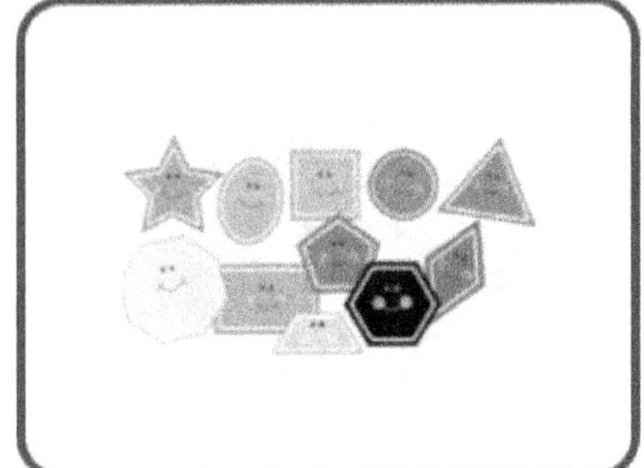

I have an interest in flowers.

shape
আকৃতি

What shape is that?

washington
ওয়াশিংটন

She is from Washington.

listen
শোনা

Do you listen to music?

spring
বসন্ত

Is it finally spring?

each
প্রতি

They were one dollar each.

ahead
এগিয়ে

Who was ahead in the race?

chief
নেতা

Is your dad the fire chief?

went
গিয়েছিলাম

We went to recess.

blue
নীল

It's a blue butterfly.

blow
ঘা

Did you blow the bubbles?

two
দুই

There are two owls.

age
বয়স

They were around the same age

bring
আনা

Bring your friends!

speak
কথা বলা

Who will speak next?

it
এটা

It is raining.

young
তরুণ

Her kids are young.

ground
স্থল

Grass covered the ground.

every
প্রতি

I shower every day.

clean
পরিষ্কার

Did you clean?

another
অন্য

Have another cookie.

laughed
অপহাসিত

They all laughed.

visit
দর্শন

They went to visit their grandparents.

hear
শোনা

You hear through your ears.

supply
সরবরাহ

Did you supply what you needed?

scientists
বিজ্ঞানীরা

They are scientists.

raised
উত্থাপিত

Everybody raised their hands.

plant
উদ্ভিদ

I will water the plant.

japanese
জাপানি

These are Japanese cherry blossoms.

country
দেশ

Do you live in the country?

to
প্রতি

I went to school.

alone
একা

While alone, he read.

verb
ক্রিয়া

Which word is a verb?

how
কিভাবে

How was the football game?

stand
থাকা

Please stand up.

metal
ধাতু

They have a metal trashcan.

room
ঘর

They hang out in this room.

products
পণ্য

Which products do you like?

branches
শাখা

There are three branches.

road
রাস্তা

Is this the right road?

circle
বৃত্ত

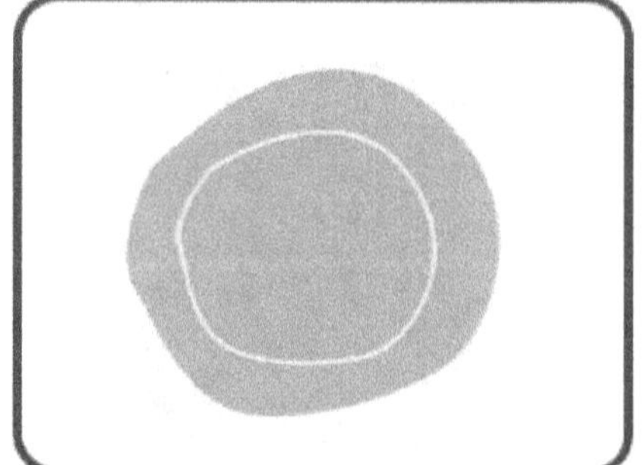

She drew a circle.

hat
টুপি

I like your new hat.

sure
নিশ্চিত

Sure, I'll go to the magic show!

seen
দেখা

Have any of you seen the movie?

pretty
চমৎকার

Pretty in pink.

name
নাম

What is his name?

practice
অনুশীলন করা

They were at practice.

horse
ঘোড়া

Have you ever ridden a horse?

matter
ব্যাপার

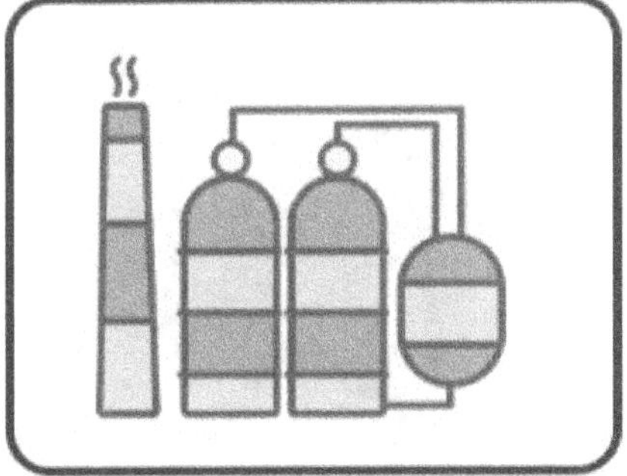

What are the states of matter?

birds
পাখি

There's a lot of birds.

things
কিছু

She washed a lot of things.

live
লাইভ দেখান

You live in the city.

caught
ধরা

You caught a fish.

we'll
আমরা হব

We'll finish buying our groceries.

pair
যুগল

Are those your pair of shoes?

work
কাজ

Hard work pays off.

scale
স্কেল

Use the scale to weigh them.

east
পূর্ব

Are you from the east coast?

solution
সমাধান

I figured out a solution!

died
মারা যান

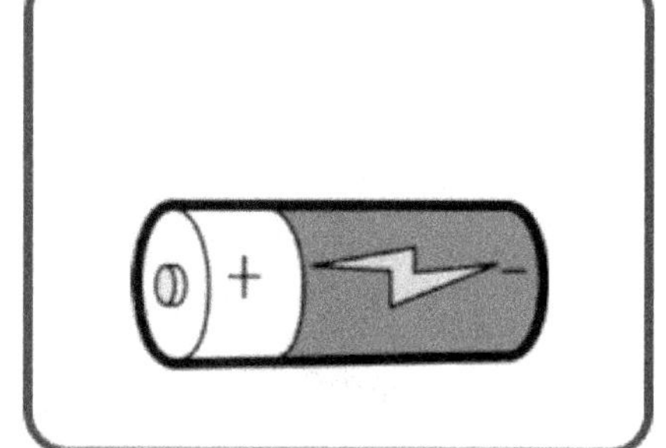

I didn't charge my phone and it died.

carry
বহন

She had a bag to carry her groceries.

sing
sing

We sing.

pulled
টানা

He pulled the wagon.

southern
দক্ষিণ

She's a southern belle.

wouldn't
হবে না

Wouldn't you like to go shopping?

let's
চল

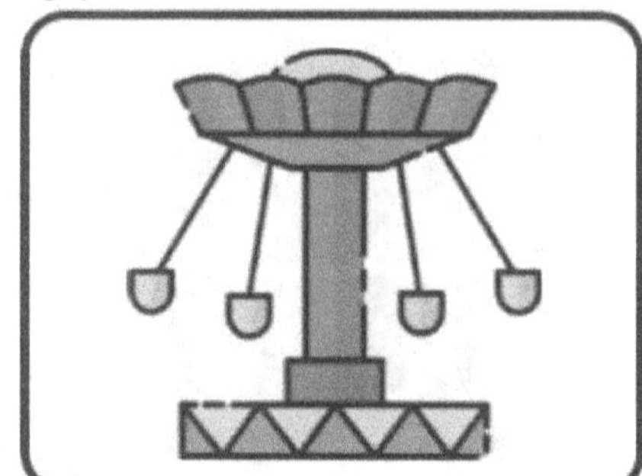

Let's go to the fair!

get
পাওয়া

Did you get your report card?

everything
সব

Everything here is fun.

use
ব্যবহার

Let's use the pool.

here
এখানে

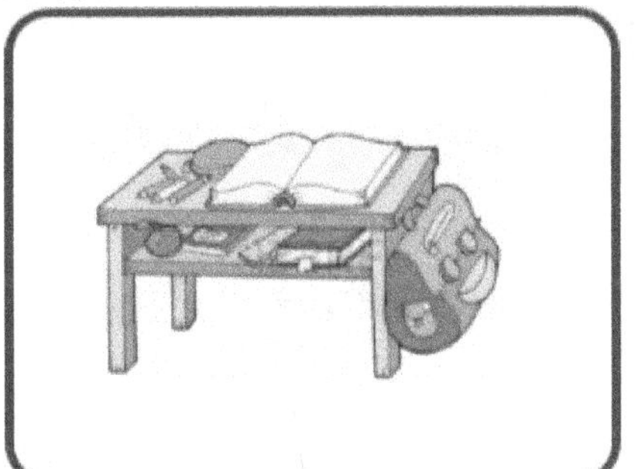

Do you sit here?

list
তালিকা

Here's my to-do list

edge
প্রান্ত

I stood at the edge of the pond.

war
যুদ্ধ

The war of the Empire and the Republic.

son
পুত্র

Is that your son?

poem
কবিতা

Would you read your poem?

some
কিছু

I need some paper.

help
সাহায্যের

You should help others.

legs
পাগুলো

A cricket has six legs.

house
গৃহ

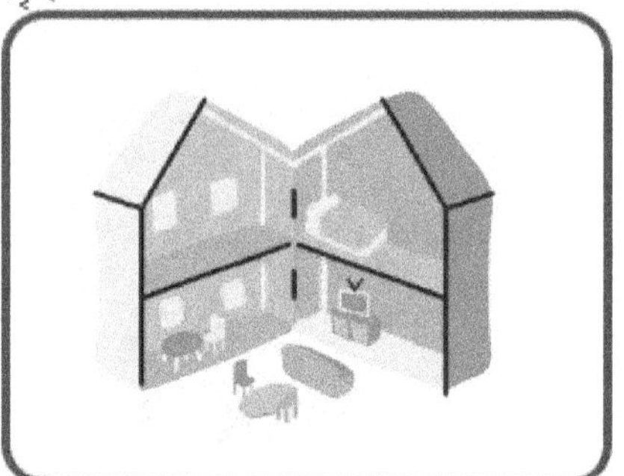

The doll house was pink.

window
জানলা

Plants are in the window.

eat
খাওয়া

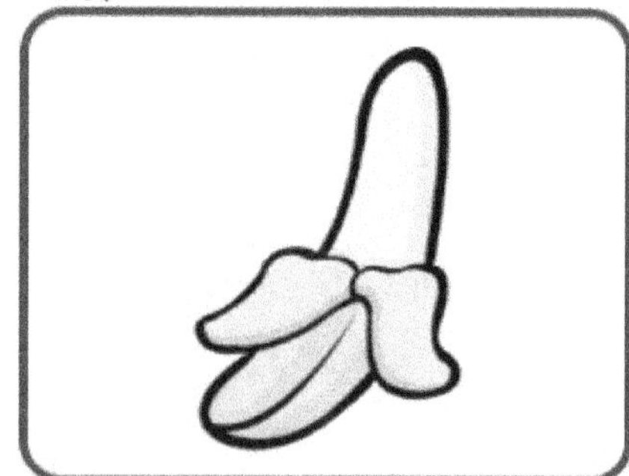

I eat bananas.

property
সম্পত্তি

That property is for sale.

grow
হওয়া

The plant began to grow.

new
নতুন

We have a new teacher.

hoe
নিড়ানি

Use a hoe in the garden.

system
পদ্ধতি

Tell me about the solar system.

hot
গরম

The coffee is hot.

within
মধ্যে

What did you see within the museum.

sister
বোন

Is she your sister?

across
দিয়ে

It's across the street.

street
রাস্তা

It's on this street.

outside
বাইরে

They brought sand in from outside.

sir
জনাব

Yes, sir!

no
না

No talking in the library.

equation
সমীকরণ

Find the answer to the equation.

be
থাকা

We'll be reading.

track
ট্র্যাক

The runners got on the track.

always
সর্বদা

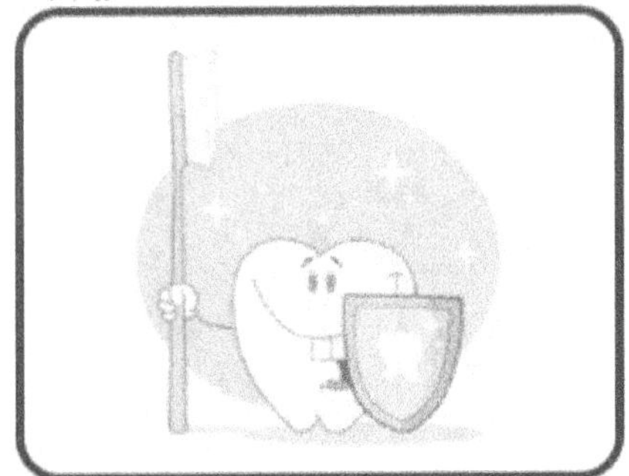

She always brushes her teeth.

length
লম্বা

What's the length?

below
নিচে

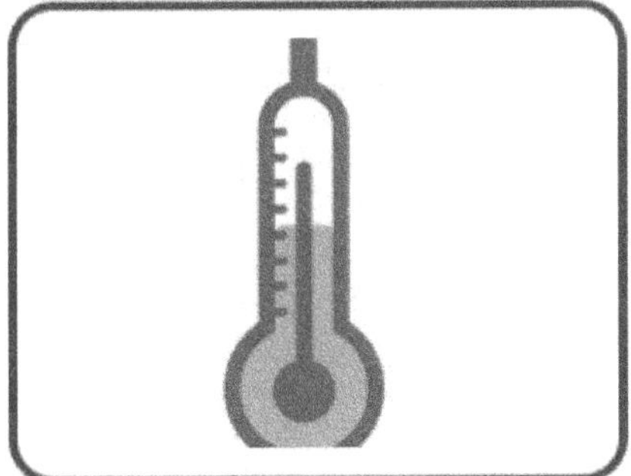

It's below thirty degrees.

everyone
সবাই

Everyone was working.

among
মধ্যে

He was among the chairs.

discovered
আবিষ্কৃত

Who discovered antibiotics?

sent
পাঠানো

Was the email sent?

yourself
নিজেকে

Did you go hiking by yourself?

cook
রাঁধুনি

What did you cook?

apple
আপেল

Eat an apple.

should
উচিত

We should exercise.

spot
অকুস্থল

It's a red spot.

plan
পরিকল্পনা

Look at the house plan.

count
গণনা

How high can you count?

printed
মুদ্রিত

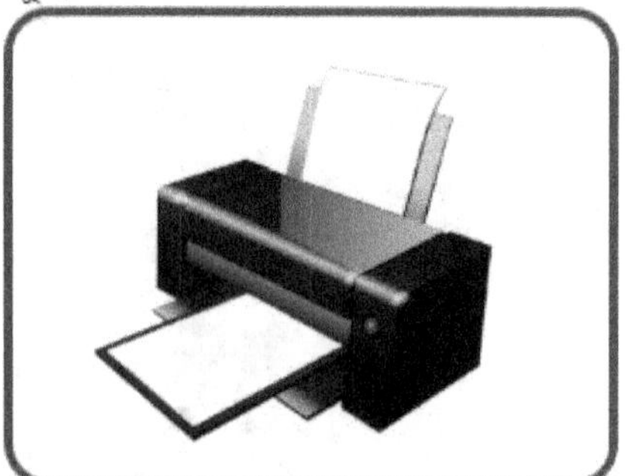

She printed out the forms.

express
প্রকাশ করা

They have express delivery.

answer
উত্তর

Raise your hand to answer.

distance
দূরত্ব

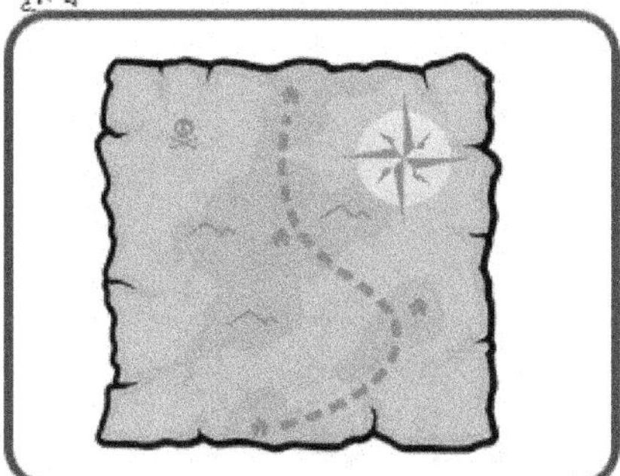

What's the distance to there?

isn't
নয়

Isn't it nice to hang out with friends?

represent
চিত্রিত করা

He drew pictures to represent words.

catch
ধরা

Did you catch the ball?

planets
গ্রহ

We were learning about the planets.

paint
রং

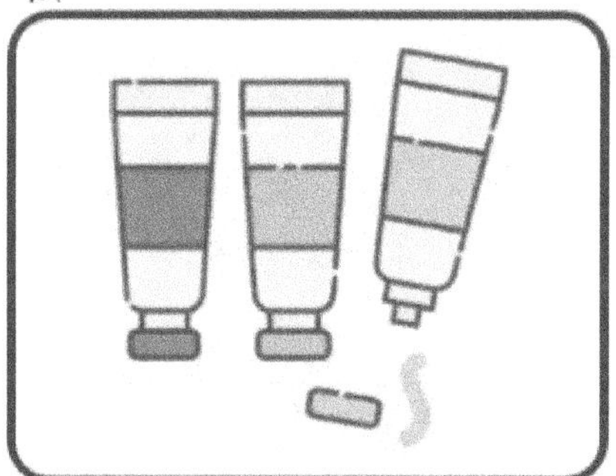

What did you paint?

ice
বরফ

The ice was melting.

through
মাধ্যম

He was through with the race.

well
আমরা হব

You did well.

shop
দোকান

I'm need to go shop for groceries.

even
এমন কি

They learned about even numbers.

god
সৃষ্টিকর্তা

Many believe in God and angels.

action
ক্রিয়াকলাপ

Action!

cool
শীতল

That's a cool car.

an
একটি

I have an idea!

fingers
আঙুলের

Cross your fingers.

row
সারি

Did you go out on row boats?

wonder
আশ্চর্যের কিছু নেই

I wonder what we'll see!

may
may

You may use the computer.

made
প্রণীত

You made an A on the test.

several
বিভিন্ন

They looked at several creatures.

and
এবং

I like cats and dogs.

ocean
মহাসাগর

I love the ocean.

game
খেলা

Who won the game?

fruit
ফল

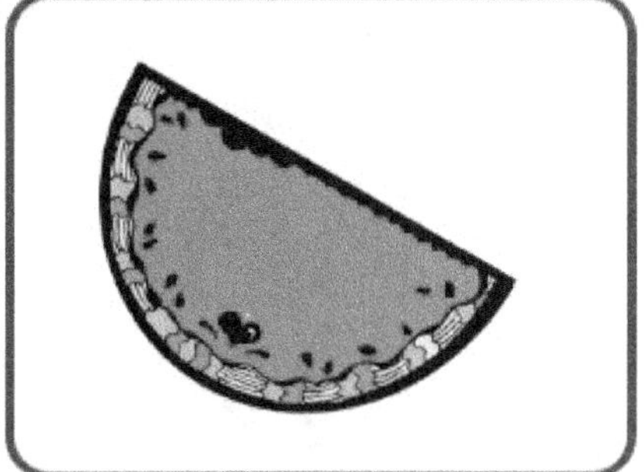

Watermelon is my favorite fruit.

process
প্রক্রিয়া

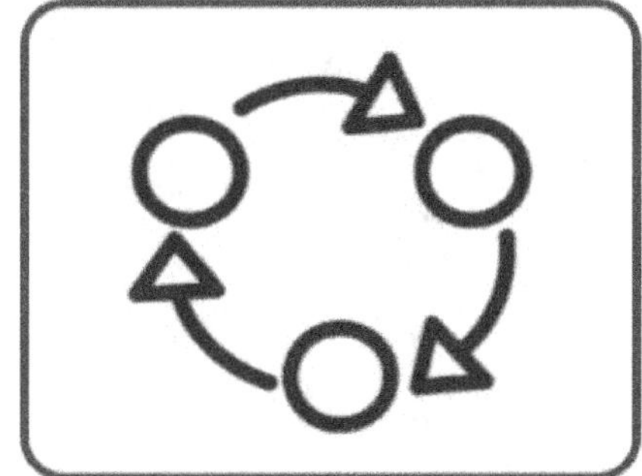

Is that the process?

current
বর্তমান

Are these your current goals?

child
শিশু

The child prayed.

my
আমার

My favorite color is blue.

tied
বাঁধা

Did you tie a knot?

arrived
আগত

My plane arrived on time.

indicate
ইঙ্গিত

Did you indicate that you are ill?

million
মিলিয়ন

She watched a million how-to videos.

law
আইন

It's the law.

finished
সমাপ্ত

He finished his painting.

found
পাওয়া

We found a puppy.

chance
সুযোগ

Dice is a game of chance.

exercise
ব্যায়াম

We all should exercise.

ring
রিং

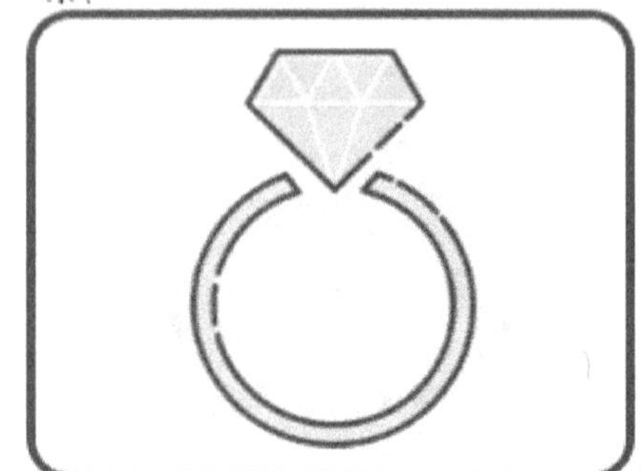

Such a beautiful ring!

view
দৃশ্য

That is a beautiful view!

separate
আলাদা

The brain has separate parts.

stop
স্টপ

Do you see the stop sign?

move
পদক্ষেপ

His family decided to move.

eyes
চোখ

What color are her eyes?

step
ধাপ

Here's the step ladder.

does
না

Does he ride the bus?

under
অধীনে

It lives under the sea.

bright
উজ্জ্বল

The sun is really bright.

learn
শেখা

It's fun to learn science.

cost
মূল্য

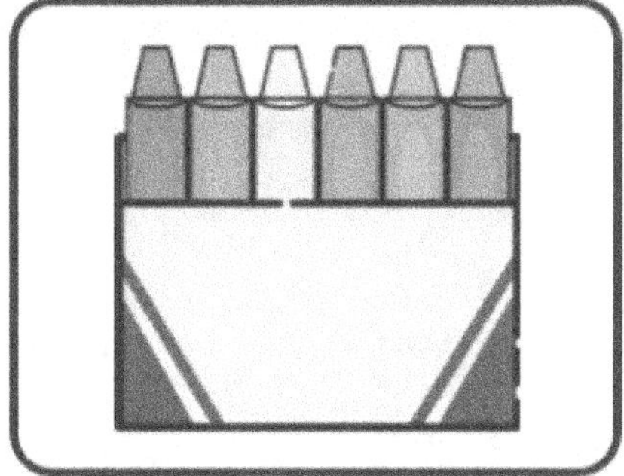

They cut the cost.

any
কোন

Do you have any crayons?

swim
সন্তরণ

Let's go for a swim!

paragraph
অনুচ্ছেদ

Have you written a paragraph?

gold
স্বর্ণ

She had a gold star.

night
রাত

You can see the stars at night.

uncle
চাচা

We learned about Uncle Sam.

seeds
বীজ

Did you get seeds for the garden?

sense
অনুভূতি

What sense did you just use?

weather
আবহাওয়া

What is the weather like?

yellow
হলুদ

A banana is yellow.

milk
দুধ

Did you drink your milk?

sky
আকাশ

The sky is clear.

take
গ্রহণ করা

Please take your seat.

baby
বাচ্চা

Is this your baby?

shouted
চিৎকার

The cheerleaders shouted their cheer.

case
কেস

Don't forget your case.

car
গাড়ী

He bought a new car.

consider
বিবেচনা

Did you consider it?

along
বরাবর

We get along.

stay
থাকা

She knows stay.

land
জমি

They bought some land.

people
সম্প্রদায়

Alot of people were dancing.

history
ইতিহাস

She taught history.

language
ভাষা

Do you know sign language?

method
পদ্ধতি

We use the scientific method.

someone
কেউ

Someone cleaned their desk.

skin
চামড়া

She used a mask for her skin.

eight
আট

Did you hit the eight ball?

born
জন্ম

Where were you born?

radio
রেডিও

Let's listen to the radio.

around
কাছাকাছি

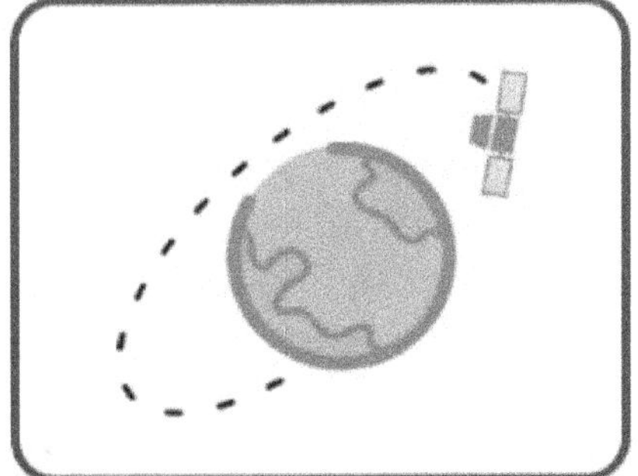

Let's travel around the world.

science
বিজ্ঞান

We love science.

check
চেক

Did you get a check mark?

desert
মরুভূমি

Have you been to the desert?

expect
আশা করা

When do you expect the baby?

behind
পিছনে

The cow was behind the fence.

object
উদ্দেশ্য

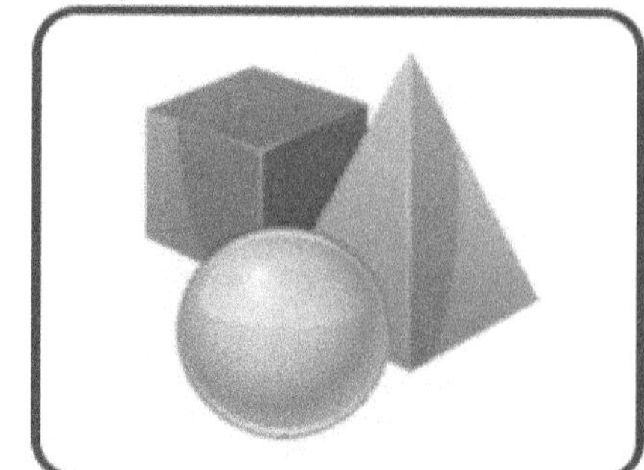

We measured each object.

tall
লম্বা

How tall is a giraffe?

but
কিন্তু

I like peas, but not cabbage.

red
লাল

It's a red heart.

slowly
ধীরে ধীরে

The turtle walked slowly.

lot
অনেক

The car lot was full.

sell
বিক্রয়

She is going to sell lemonade.

interesting
মজাদার

The dog thought the toy was interesting.

while
যখন

We had fun while skiing.

thus
এইভাবে

I was tired, thus I didn't go to the party.

belong
অন্তর্গত

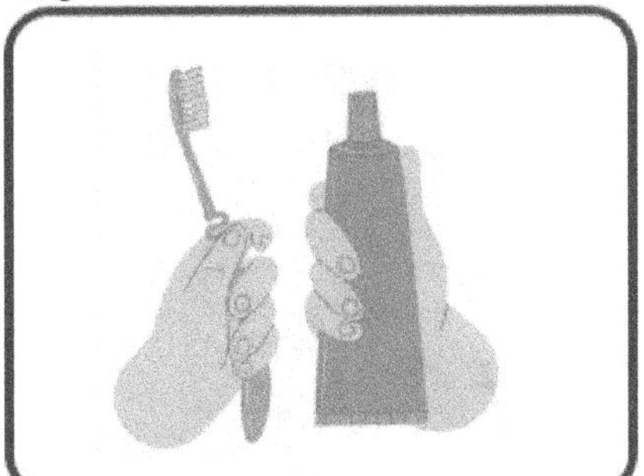

They belong together.

score
স্কোর

What was the final score?

inches
উচ্চতা

How many inches is it?

with
সঙ্গে

He had toast with his cereal.

send
পাঠান

Did you send the letter?

train
রেলগাড়ি

We have a Christmas train.

create
সৃষ্টি

What art did you create?

who
কে

Who likes hockey?

shown
প্রদার্শিত

The photo was shown to me.

feet
পা দুটো

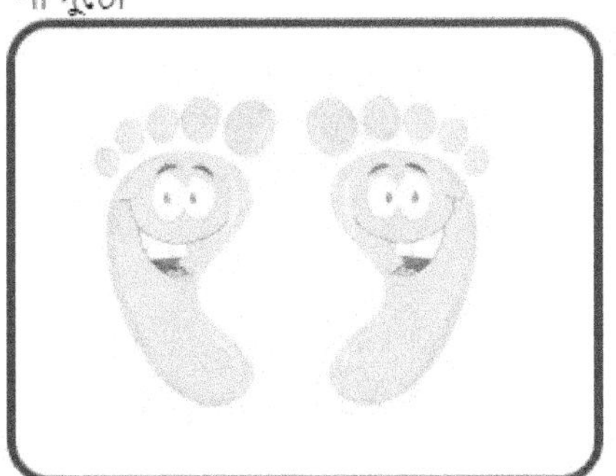

Put socks on your feet.

industry
শিল্প

This is where the industry is.

sign
চিহ্ন

There's a stop sign.

provide
প্রদান

We wanted to provide food.

tree
গাছ

Did you decorate the tree?

allow
অনুমতি

Did the teacher allow him to go play?

hill
পাহাড়

The sun peaked over the hill.

too
অত্যাধিক

Do you like chocolate too?

rhythm
তাল

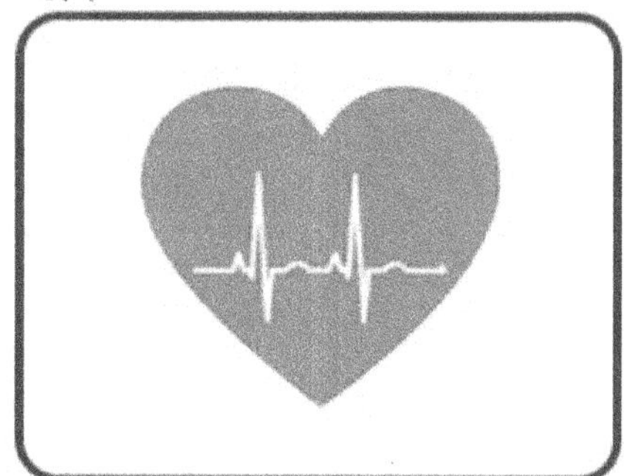

That's your heart's rhythm.

dress
পোশাক

She loved her new dress.

many
অনেক

How many are in the jar?

give
দিতে

I like to give gifts.

five
পাঁচ

There are five of them.

western
পশ্চিম

It's western wear day.

was
ছিল

She was reading.

able
সক্ষম

Are you able to ride a bike?

heart
হৃদয়

Did you draw a heart?

particular
বিশেষ

I prefer a particular ketchup.

ball
বল

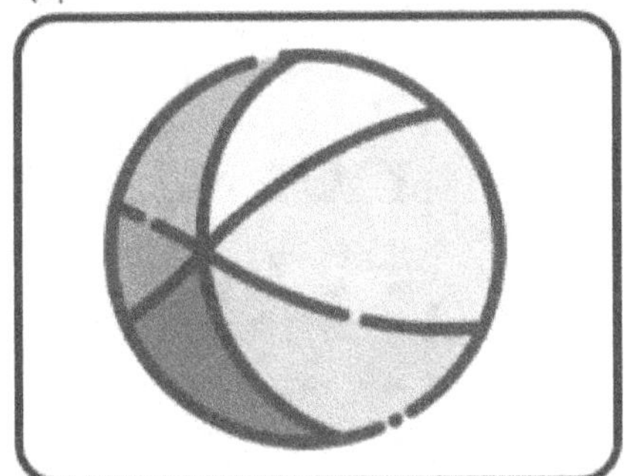

He was among the chairs.

first
প্রথম

He earned first place.

wrote
লিখেছেন

She wrote poetry

held
অনুষ্ঠিত

They held hands.

lady
ভদ্রমহিলা

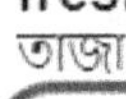

The lady worked long hours.

fresh
তাজা

All the fruit is fresh.

shoulder
অংস

Did you hurt your shoulder?

known
পরিচিত

They've known each other forever.

need
প্রয়োজন

Do you need to sleep?

man
মানুষ

The man drove.

wrong
ভুল

Did I get it wrong?

away
দূরে

Throw your trash away.

anything
কিছু

Do cows eat anything but grass?

flowers
ফুল

Flowers are growing there.

buy
কেনা

Did you buy a new car?

least
অন্তত

Did you at least remember your bag?

flow
প্রবাহ

We created a flow chart.

both
উভয়

They both worked on math.

sum
সমষ্টি

What is the sum of this?

third
তৃতীয়

How did you like third grade?

said
বললেন

She said hello.

from
থেকে

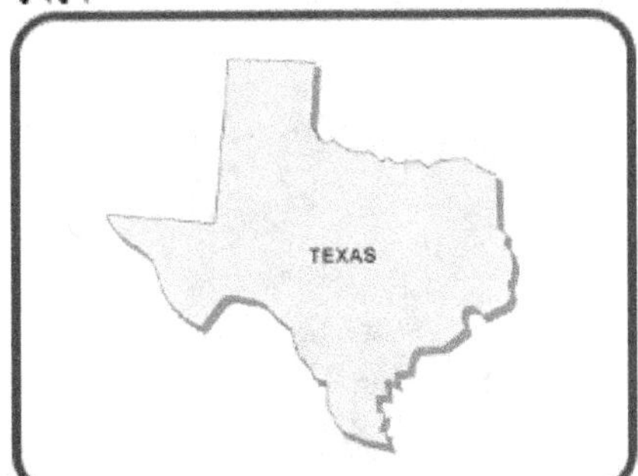

I am from Texas.

entire
সমগ্র

The entire family was in the picture.

head
মাথা

He wore a cap on his head.

important
গুরুত্বপূর্ণ

It's important!

beautiful
সুন্দর

The area is beautiful.

his
তার

It's his soccer ball.

arms
অস্ত্র

She crossed her arms.

left
বাম

Are you left or right handed?

door
দরজা

The door was open.

music
সঙ্গীত

I love music.

not
না

A giraffe is not short.

had
ছিল

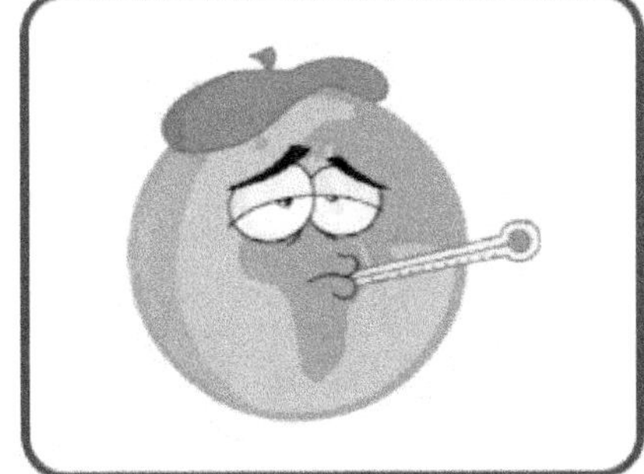

Mrs. Smith had a cold.

done
সম্পন্ন

Well done!

can't
নারা

When I can't sleep, I count sheep.

feel
অনুভব করা

How do you feel?

note
বিঃদ্রঃ

She left a note.

come
আসা

Will you come to the park?

coast
উপকূল

The coast is relaxing.

position
অবস্থান

She likes sitting in that position.

thought
চিন্তার

I thought the novel was good.

cattle
গবাদি পশু

We raise cattle.

rise
ওঠা

We were waiting for the sun to rise.

stood
দাঁড়িয়ে

He stood at the teacher's desk.

sound
শব্দ

A bee makes a buzzing sound.

open
খোলা

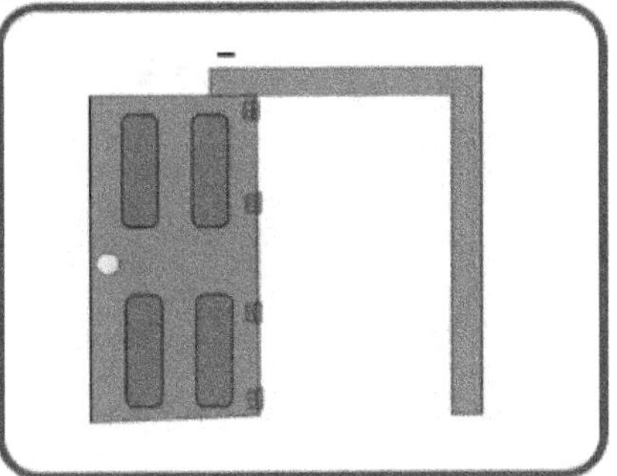

The door is open.

six
ছয়

He rolled a six.

fair
মজাদার পার্ক

Let's go to the fair.

lay
লে

Will she lay an egg?

hold
রাখা

Hold on to the balloons!

space
নিসর্গ

The astronaut went to space.

gone
সর্বস্বান্ত

Has he gone fishing?

questions
প্রশ্ন

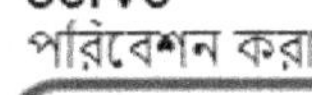

Do you have questions?

serve
পরিবেশন করা

Did you serve that table?

factories
কারখানা

There are a lot of factories there.

cat
বিড়াল

I adopted a cat.

best
সেরা

Do your best!

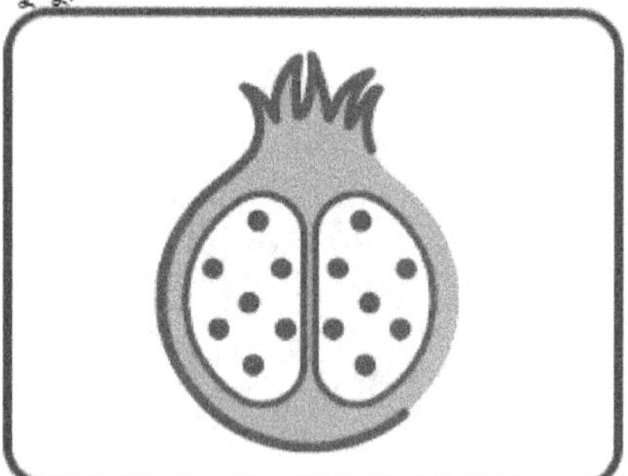

fig
ডুমুর

I ate a fig.

your
তোমার

Your ball is here.

rope
দড়ি

Do you have any rope?

know
জানা

I don't know.

back
পেছনে

We went back to school.

oil
তেল

I changed the oil in my car.

thousands
হাজার হাজার

Thousands of people live here.

mine
খনি

Be mine.

only
কেবল

There's only one slice left.

couldn't
না পারা

Couldn't we throw a fundraiser?

began
শুরু হয়

The baby began to cry.

effect
প্রভাব

How did the medicine effect your cold?

lost
নিখোঁজ

Have you lost something?

cause
কারণ

What's the cause?

reached
পৌঁছে

You reached high for your goals.

you
আপনি

You are strong.

morning
সকাল

Do you drink coffee in the morning?

play
খেলা

Let's play together!

don't
না

Don't forget!

feeling
অনুভূতি

He's feeling sick.

present
বর্তমান

Who is the present for?

area
এলাকায়

There are no wild animals in this area.

for
জন্য

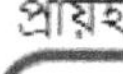

We ate turkey for Thanksgiving.

often
প্রায়ই

How often do you watch tv?

sat
শান

They sat and listened.

northern
উত্তর

He lives in northern California.

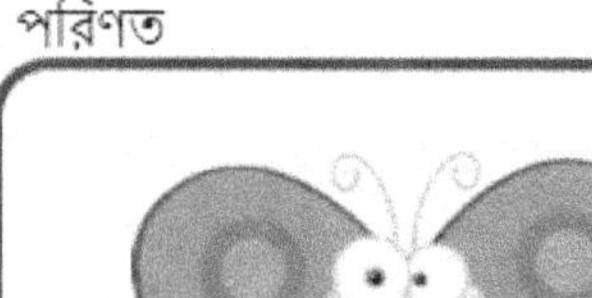

become
পরিণত

It will become a butterfly.

above
উপরে

The sky was above them.

town
শহর

Meet at the town square.

eggs
ডিম

Do you have enough eggs?

without
ছাড়া

I can't go without my backpack.

ship
জাহাজ

The ship sailed.

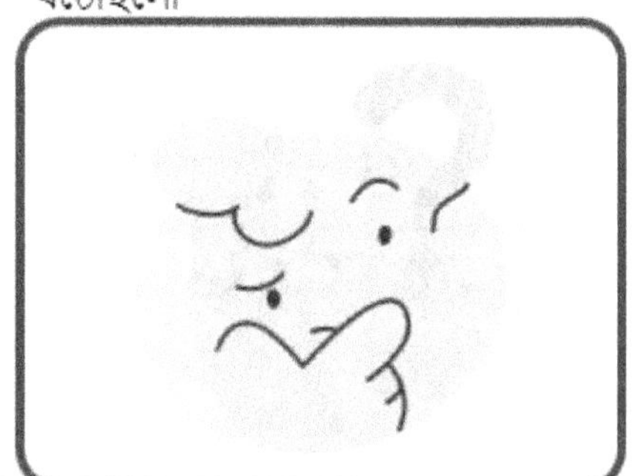

happened
ঘটেছিলো

What happend?

weight
ওজন

The scale will measure your weight.

natural
প্রাকৃতিক

This place has natural beauty.

report
প্রতিবেদন

Your report card looks great!

total
মোট

What's the total?

mother
মা

He loves his mother.

decimal
দশমিক

Where does the decimal go?

ride
অশ্বারোহণ

Let's ride bikes!

nothing
কিছু না

He had nothing he had to do.

doctor
ডাক্তার

He went to see the doctor.

inside
ভিতরে

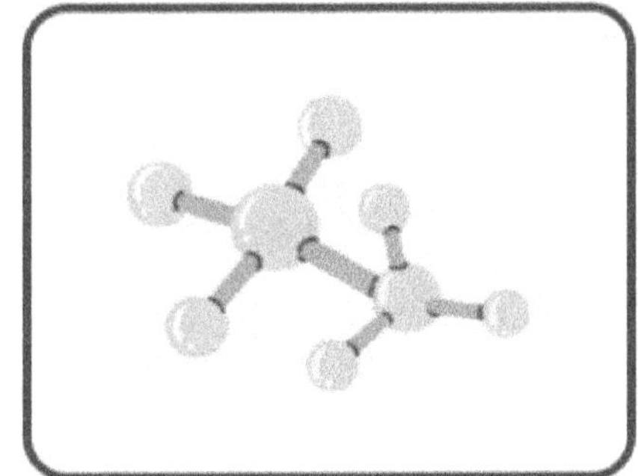

He was inside the dog house.

reason
কারণ

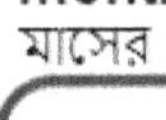

Science uses logic and reason.

months
মাসের

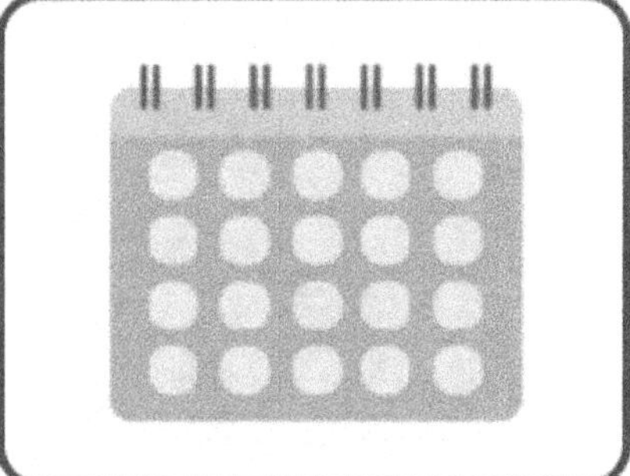

There are several cold months.

general
সাধারণ

We shopped at the general store.

set
সেট

Please set the table.

words
শব্দ

You make words to play.

jumped
jumped

The cow jumped over the moon.

meet
সম্মেলন

Do you want to meet them?

find
অনুসন্ধান

Did you find your keys?

yard
গজ

Lucky is in the yard.

walk
পদব্রজে ভ্রমণ

We went for a walk.

course
পথ

Did you go to the golf course?

afraid
ভীত

What are you afraid of?

angle
কোণ

Please measure the angle.

appear
প্রদর্শিত

You appear to be lost.

noun
বিশেষ্য

Is that a noun or a verb?

please
অনুগ্রহ

Please have breakfast.

white
সাদা

They drew on the white board.

picture
ছবি

They took their picture.

if
যদি

If you are sick, go see the nurse.

flat
সমান

The tire was flat.

can
করতে পারা

Can you go to the zoo?

government
সরকার

We learned about the government.

level
উচ্চতা

Use the level to hang the picture.

melody
সুর

What a beautiful melody.

experience
অভিজ্ঞতা

She has a lot of experience.

table
টেবিল

Please sit at the table.

us
আমাদের

She taught us.

between
মধ্যে

Two is between one and three.

syllables
সিলাবল

We are working on syllables.

came
এল

He came to class.

in
ভিতরে

Halloween is in October.

short
সংক্ষিপ্ত

You cut your hair short.

bought
কিনলেন

She bought new clothes.

led
এলইডউ

The dog led her.

build
বিল্ড

What are you going to build?

century
শতাব্দী

They said it's a century old.

necessary
প্রয়োজনীয়

It is necessary to go to school.

stick
লাঠি

It's your hockey stick.

shoes
জুতা

Put your shoes on.

climbed
আরোহন

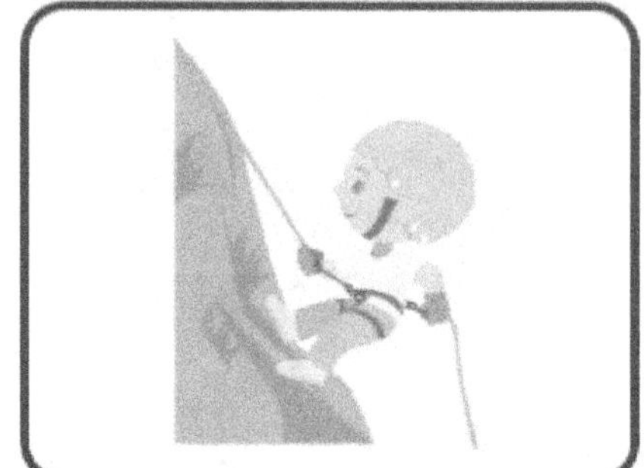

They climbed it.

settled
স্থায়ী

The case was settled.

family
পরিবার

How big is your family?

continued
অব্যাহত

He continued to look through the box.

africa
আফ্রিকা

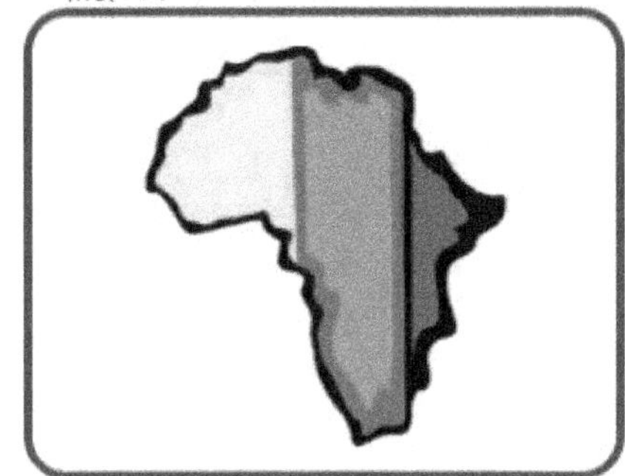

Did you vist Southern Africa?

this
এই

This is your backpack.

office
দপ্তর

Do you need any office supplies?

control
নিয়ন্ত্রণ

Who has the remote control?

whole
গোটা

Were you sick the whole time?

where
কোথায়

Where do you want to go?

upon
উপরে

Once upon a time there was a princess.

information
তথ্য

He took in so much information.

repeated
পুনরাবৃত্ত

They repeated the exercises daily.

moment
মুহূর্ত

Wait a moment for the bus.

voice
কণ্ঠস্বর

Use your quiet voice.

large
বড়

A bear is large.

river
নদী

The river is high.

block
বাধা

Did you have a toy block?

match
ম্যাচ

Did you match them?

else
আর

Did you draw that or did someone else?

called
নামক

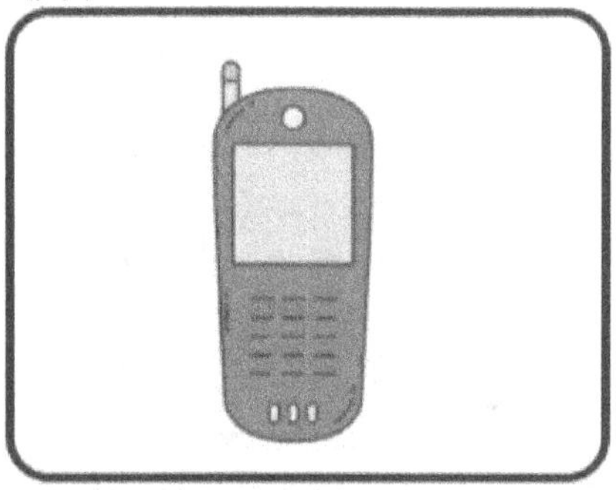

I need to call my mom

mouth
মুখ

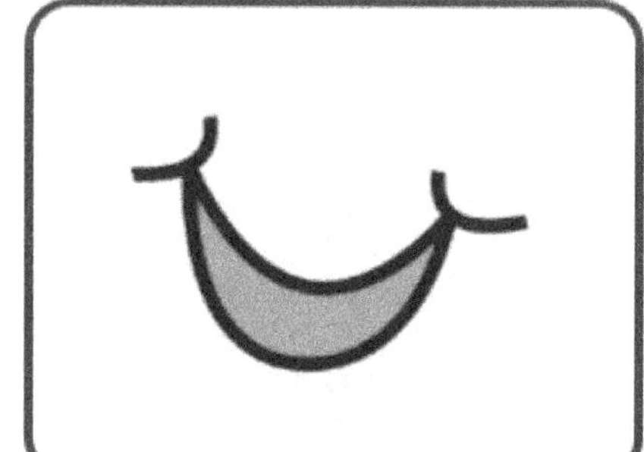

Do your braces make your mouth hurt?

site
সাইট

Have you looked at the site?

material
উপাদান

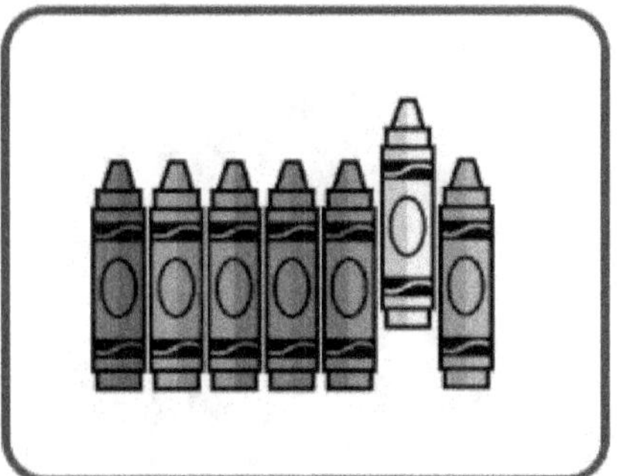

She needed material.

chart
তালিকা

What does your medical chart say?

cells
কোষ

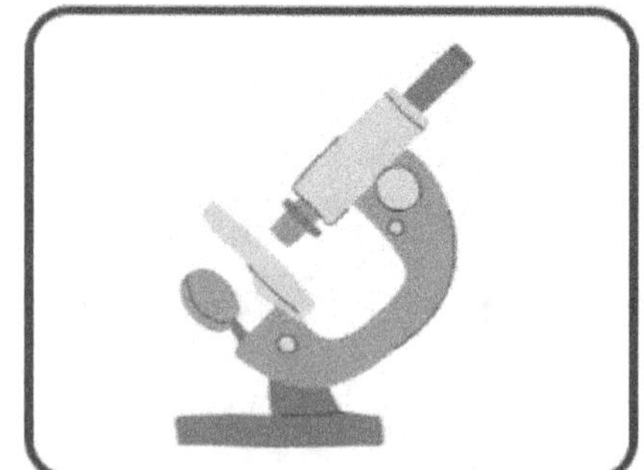

We learned about cells.

won't
না করবে না

Won't you go fishing with me?

wish
ইচ্ছা

Make a wish!

soil
মাটি

Plant it in the soil.

except
ছাড়া

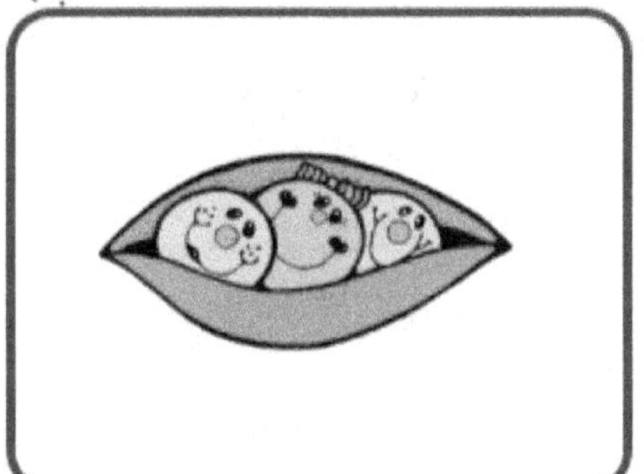

like all vegetables except peas.

past
গত

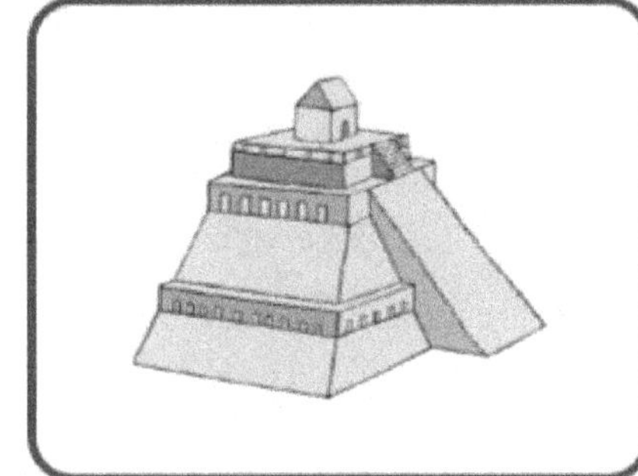

Archeology looks at the past.

dead
মৃত

The bug is dead.

teacher
শিক্ষক

The teacher read to them.

right
অধিকার

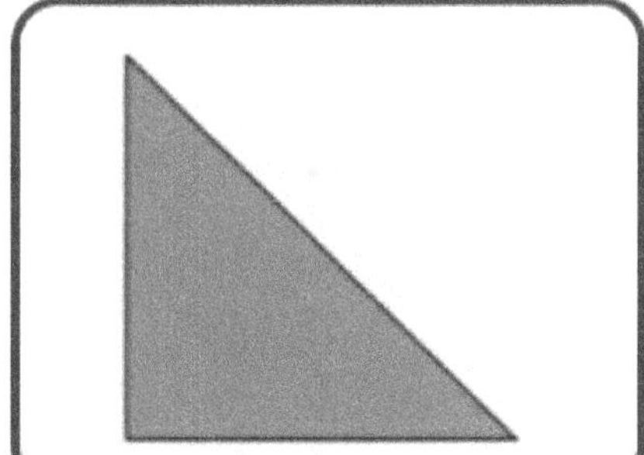

That's a right triangle.

deep
গভীর

The ocean is very deep.

beside
পাশে

They stood beside one another.

felt
অনুভূত

He felt happy with friends.

sail
পাল

Do you like to sail?

surface
পৃষ্ঠতল

Most of the Earth's surface is water.

look
বর্ণন

Let's look at the stars.

church
গির্জা

Did you go to church?

common
সাধারণ

They have a lot in common.

is
হয়

It is hot outside

warm
উষ্ণ

How warm is the soup?

fish
মাছ

Do you like fish?

strong
শক্তিশালী

How strong are you?

long
দীর্ঘ

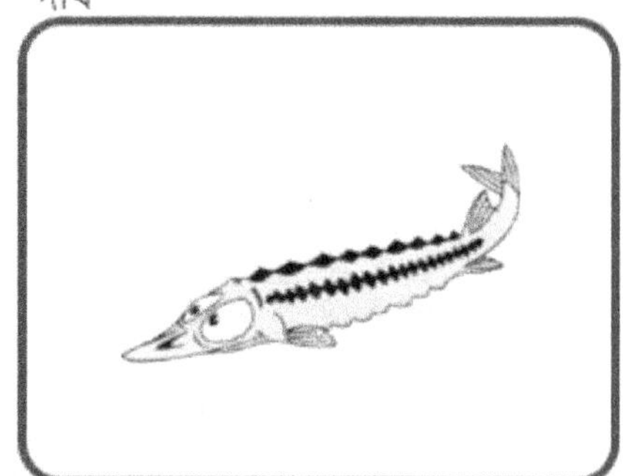

How long is it?

form
ফর্ম

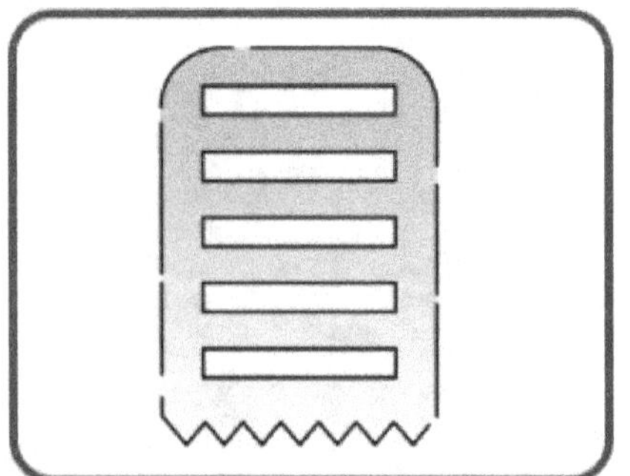

Complete the form.

describe
বর্ণনা করা

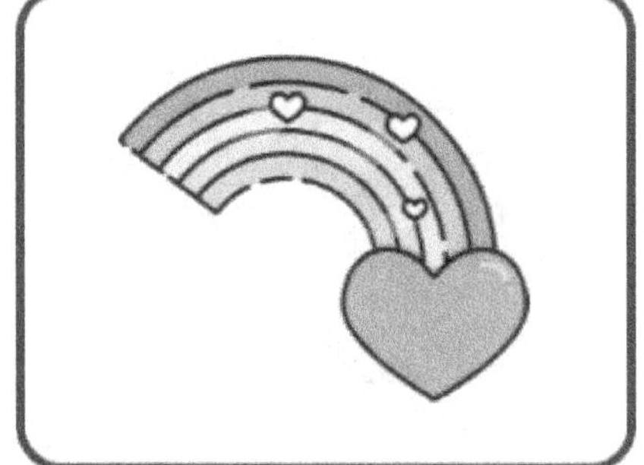

Describe the colors.

capital
রাজধানী

The capital is in Washington DC.

plains
সমভূমি

The road went through the plains

sleep
ঘুম

It's time to sleep.

stone
পাথর

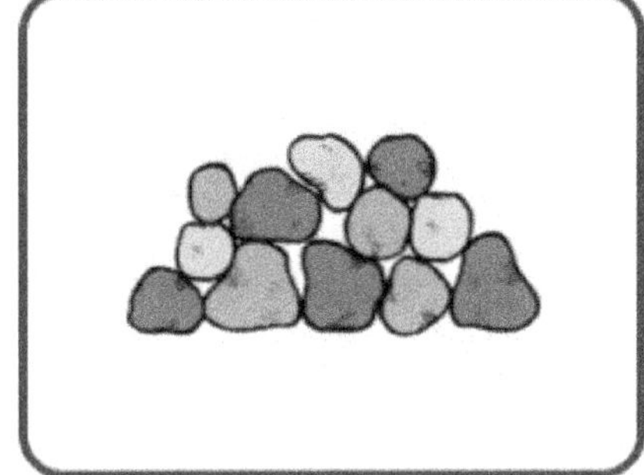

She skipped a stone across the pond.

clear
পরিষ্কার

The glass is clear.

pay
বেতন

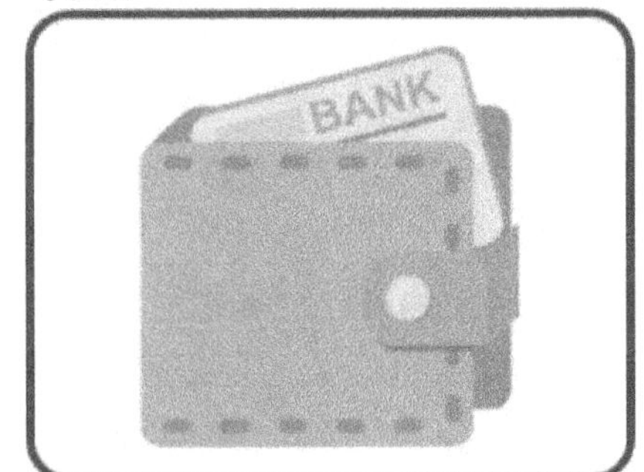

We need to pay

fell
খোলস

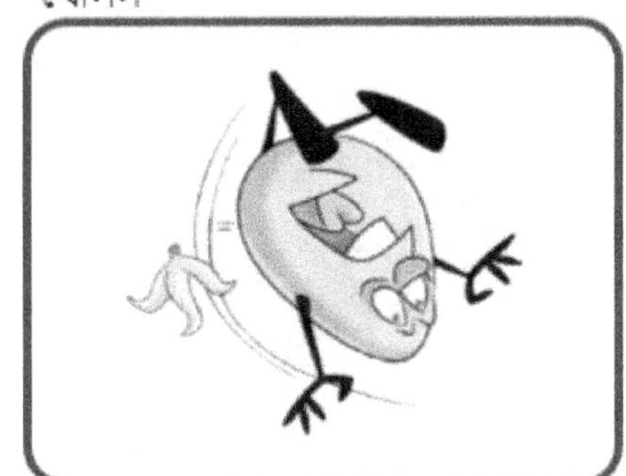

I fell down the stairs.

foot
পা

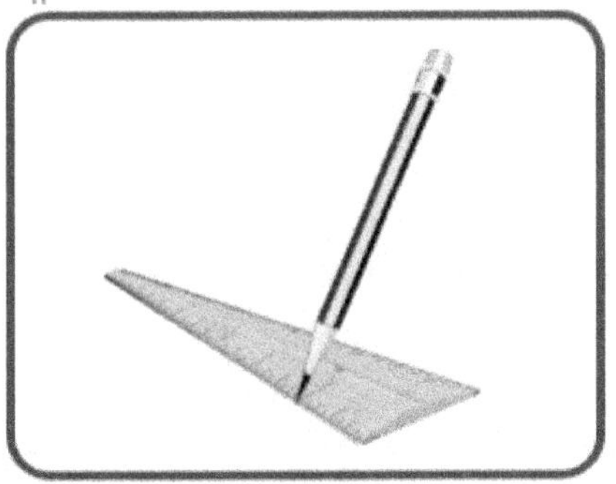

Twelve inches is a foot.

silent
নীরব

Please be silent in the library.

quickly
দ্রুত

The greyhound ran quickly.

village
গ্রাম

We travled to the village.

down
নিচে

We walked down the stairs.

correct
ঠিক

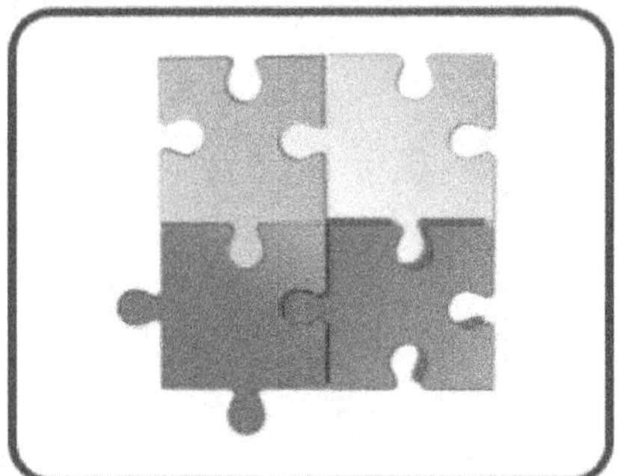

Was that the correct piece?

shall
হইবে

I shall ride this.

which
যেটি

Which snack do you want?

wasn't
ছিল না

Wasn't that your cousin?

at
এ

You're at school.

bill
বিল

Did you receive the bill?

dog
কুকুর

My dog is cute.

key
মূল

Did you find your key?

travel
ভ্রমণ

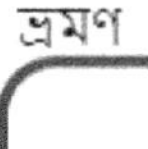

Let's travel.

maybe
হতে পারে

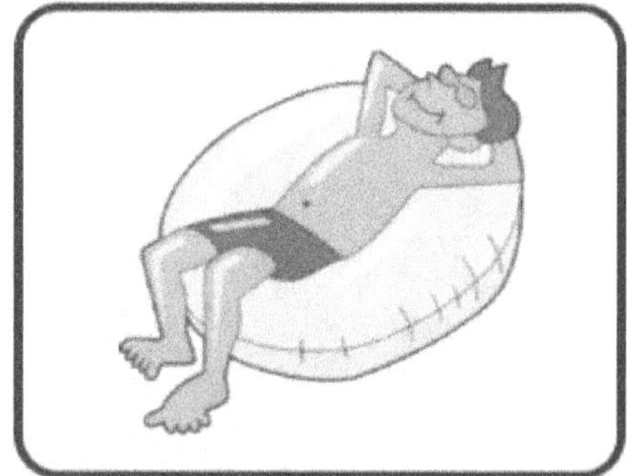

Maybe we'll go rafting.

plane
সমতল

Is it your first time on a plane?

leave
ছুটি

He packed to leave.

complete
সম্পূর্ণ

Did you complete your workout?

per
প্রতি

It's forty dollars per car.

start
শুরু

Start writing.

enjoy
উপভোগ

Did you enjoy your coffee?

has
হয়েছে

Lily has a cat.

stretched
টানা

We stretched before the workout.

exactly
ঠিক

It was exactly as she imagined.

job
কাজ

What job did you chose?

cannot
না পারেন

You cannot succeed without hard work.

england
ইংল্যান্ড

I want to go to England.

pattern
প্যাটার্ন

Which dress pattern?

experiment
পরীক্ষা

What was your experiment?

adjective
বিশেষণ

Tell me an adjective to describe this.

when
কখন

When is the dance?

big
বৃহৎ

The elephant is a big animal.

wood
কাঠ

Did you chop the wood?

knew
জানতাম

She knew the doctor.

say
বলে

What did you say?

letter
চিঠি

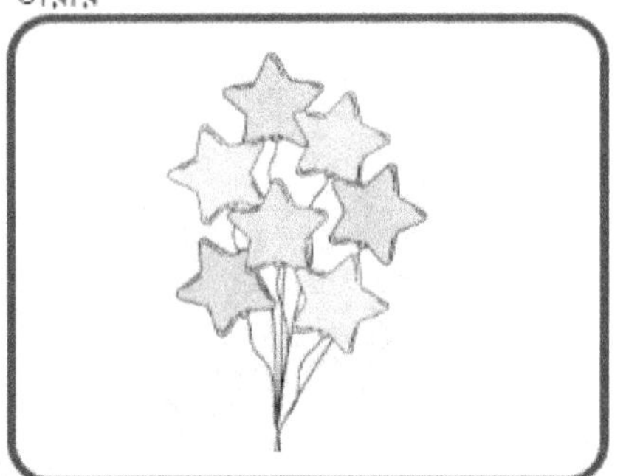

He mailed a letter.

stars
তারার

How many stars did you earn?

high
উচ্চ

She wore high heels.

gun
বন্দুক

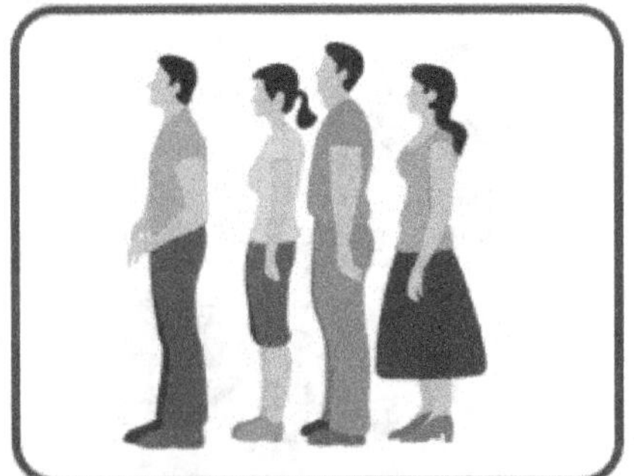

We played with a water gun.

line
লাইন

Please form a line.

joined
যোগদান

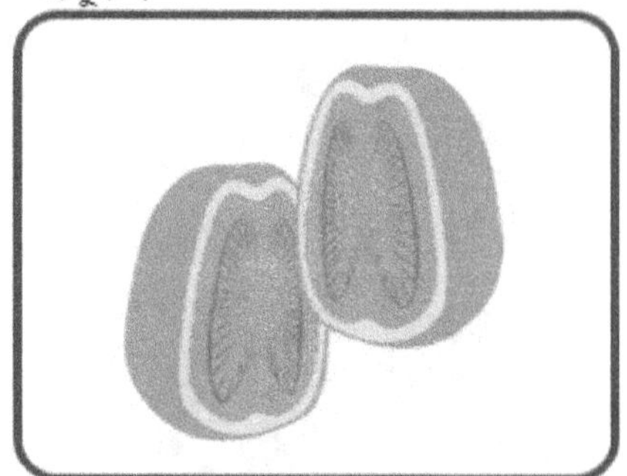

I joined them at the cafe.

similar
অনুরূপ

The halves are similar.

paper
কাগজ

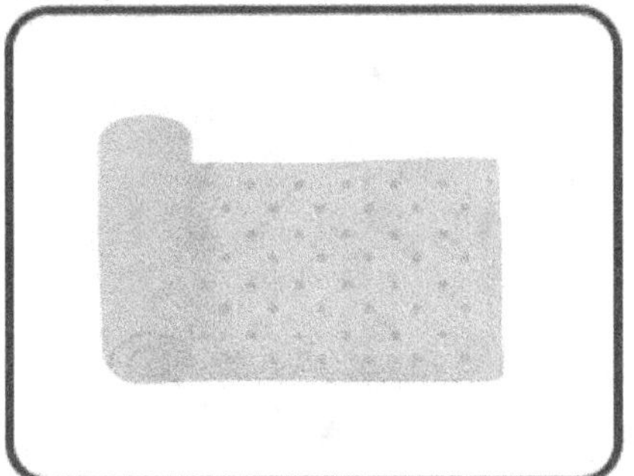

Do you have paper towels?

grass
ঘাস

Will you cut the grass?

tube
নল

That's my tube of toothpaste.

solve
সমাধান

Did you solve the equation?

tone
স্বন

He said he's tone deaf.

built
নির্মিত

He built a house.

perhaps
সম্ভবত

Perhaps you want to go in it?

evening
সন্ধ্যা

The ceremony was this evening.

compare
তুলনা করা

You can't compare apples to oranges.

order
ক্রম

Put them in order of date.

why
কেন

She asked why?

rolled
ঘূর্ণিত

The diploma was rolled up.

story
গল্প

What's the story about?

ask
জিজ্ঞাসা করা

It's good to ask questions.

killed
নিহত

Pest control killed the bugs.

straight
সোজা

It's a straight road.

then
তারপর

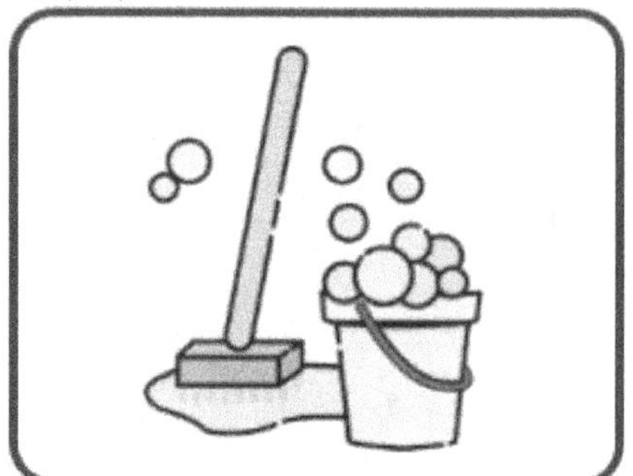

Do your chores, then you can play.

type
আদর্শ

What type of project is it?

west
পশ্চিম

You need to go west.

triangle
ত্রিভুজ

How many sides does a triangle have?

power
ক্ষমতা

What super power do you have?

add
যোগ

If you add one plus two, you get three.

hit
হিট

They hit up a lot of stores.

last
গত

It's the last day of school.

english
ইংরেজি

Do you enjoy English class?

produce
উৎপাদন করা

It will produce vegetables.

include
অন্তর্ভুক্ত করা

They made sure to include sunscreen.

bit
বিট

I bit the apple.

run
চালান

He likes to run with his dog.

against
বিরুদ্ধে

It's against the rules.

workers
শ্রমিকদের

The workers were busy.

europe
ইউরোপ

Are you going to visit Europe?

real
বাস্তব

Her real name is Sally.

side
পাশ

Each side of a square is the same.

point
বিন্দু

Point the way.

moon
চাঁদ

The wolf howled at the moon.

you're
তুমি

You're an angel.

thin
পাতলা

That's a thin book.

sit
বসা

She decided to sit.

cloud
মেঘ

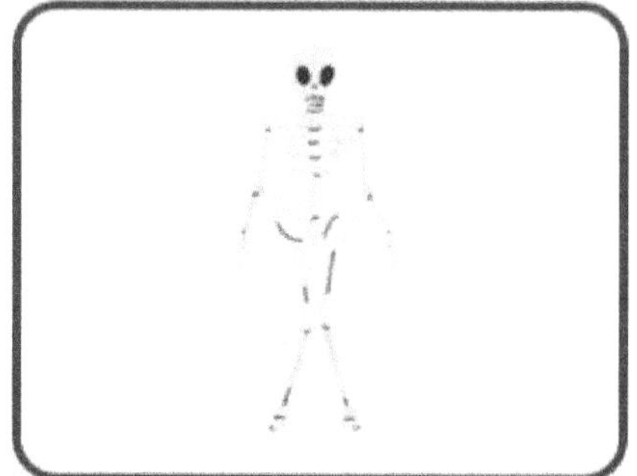

We watched the storm cloud.

human
মানবীয়

We learned about the human body.

north
উত্তর

Go north.

notice
বিজ্ঞপ্তি

Put the notice on the board.

gave
দিলেন

He gave her flowers.

ears
কান

Did you get your ears pierced?

will
ইচ্ছাশক্তি

I will go to the park.

because
কারণ

I went to bed because I was tired.

person
ব্যাক্তি

He's a smart person.

gas
গ্যাস

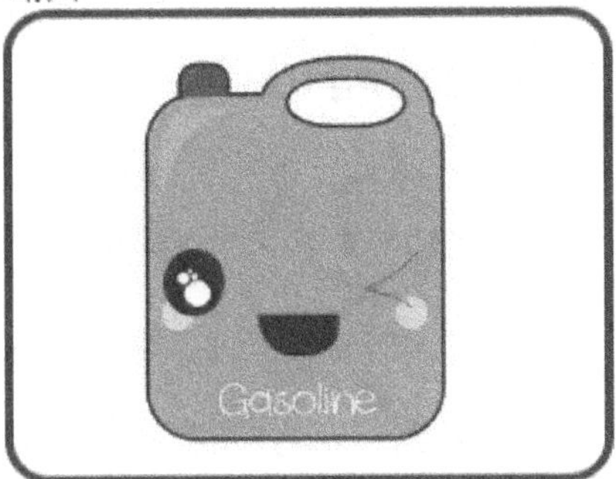

We stopped to get gas.

now
এখন

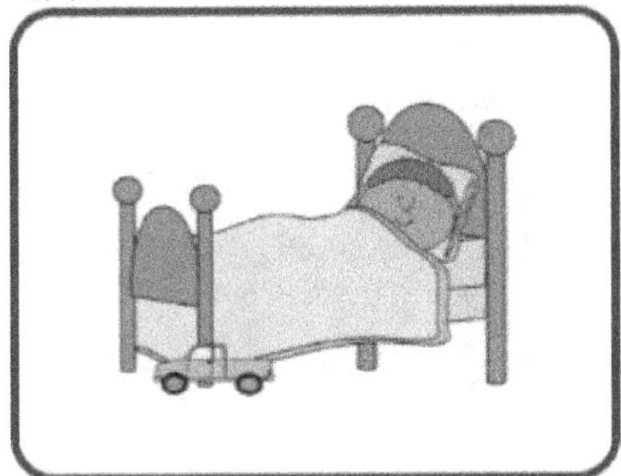

It's bedtime now.

make
করতে

We will make dinner.

dollars
ডলার

How many hundreds of dollars is it?

instruments
যন্ত্র

What instruments do you play?

increase
বৃদ্ধি

Did the house value increase?

dictionary
অভিধান

You may use a dictionary.

love
ভালবাসা

Families love each other.

wall
প্রাচীর

She painted the wall.

have
আছে

Do you have a pencil?

direction
অভিমুখ

Which direction do we go?

such
এমন

He is such a good dog.

conditions
পরিবেশ

What are the weather conditions.

late
বিলম্বে

You're late.

four
চার

There were four of them.

money
টাকা

How much money have you saved?

school
বিদ্যালয়

Do you like school?

green
সবুজ

The frog is green.

drawing
অঙ্কন

Is that your drawing?

guess
অনুমান

Guess how many

picked
অবাচিত

They picked the book together.

waves
ঢেউখেলানো

The waves were great for surfing.

today
আজ

Today we'll go to the pool.

major
মুখ্য

What's your college major?

death মরণ	**themselves** নিজেদের	**cross** ক্রস

The grim reaper is death.	They enjoyed themselves.	There's a cross on the church.

Sample for this book

one

The panda says one.

one   one

one

our

This is our room.

our   our

our

out

He will go out.

out   out

out

own

The man owns a computer.

own   own

own

Dolch & Fry Sight Words : Read Trace Write Handbook

a

This is a bird.

a a

a

I

I will play with the toys.

i i

i

am

I am crawling on the ground.

am am

am

an

This is an ant.

an an

an

as

It is as light as a feather.

as   as

as

at

She is at her friend's house.

at   at

at

be

We will be friends.

be   be

be

by

This story is by me.

by   by

by

pig

She is sleeping on her pig.

pig   pig

pig

put

She is putting an arm around her daughter.

put   put

put

ran

She ran back home.

ran   ran

ran

red

The bus is red.

red   red

red

do

She will do the cleaning.

go

He will go somewhere.

he

He is bored.

if

If I put my clothes here, it will get washed.

Dolch & Fry Sight Words : Read Trace Write Handbook

in

The baby is in the bath.

is

The cat is happy.

it

It is my toy.

me

It's me.

my

This is my nose.

my my

my

no

No, I will not!

no no

no

of

One of the boys is my son.

of of

of

on

He turns on the light.

on on

on

or

Should I eat this or that?

so

This is so yummy.

to

She will read to the end.

up

He stacks the blocks upper.

us

Both of us are walking.

us   us

us

we

We are helping to make a house.

we   we

we

all

We are all dancing together.

all   all

all

and

My brother and I are playing.

and   and

and

any

They can read any books.

any

any

are

The eggs are colorful.

are

are

ask

The girl asks a question.

ask

ask

ate

They ate yummy ice cream.

ate

ate

bed

This bed is for the baby.

bed   bed
bed

big

The bottle is huge.

big   big
big

box

The box has all my toys.

box   box
box

boy

The boy is hiding behind it.

boy   boy
boy

but

I want to go, but my son doesn't.

but   but
but

buy

He buys lots of stuff.

buy   buy
buy

can

The baby will drink milk from the can.

can   can
can

car

The car is red.

car   car
car

not

She is not feeling well.

not   not
not

now

Now I am doing my homework.

now   now
now

off

They cut off the paper.

off   off
off

old

You are one year old!

old   old
old

cat

The cat is sad.

cat   cat

cat

cow

The cow is funny.

cow   cow

cow

cut

They are cutting out paper.

cut   cut

cut

day

This day is the 30th.

day   day

day

Month
30

her

She has her trolley.

her   her

her

him

I gave my hat to him.

him   him

him

his

His cheeks are big.

his   his

his

hot

It is hot on the beach.

hot   hot

hot

man

The man is a vet.

man   man

man

may

May I have more?

may   may

may

men

The men are mining for gold.

men   men

men

new

She has a new hat.

new   new

new

eye

The fox is closing his eyes.

eye   eye
eye

far

He can fly the plane very far.

far   far
far

fly

The bee will fly back home.

fly   fly
fly

for

The dog is begging for food.

for   for
for

get

He will get a trophy.

get   get

get

got

The baby got some new toys.

got   got

got

had

He had a big tummy.

had   had

had

has

She has a doll.

has   has

has

how

How many blocks are there?

how how
how

its

Its legs are short.

its its
its

leg

His legs are short.

leg leg
leg

let

Let me come in!

let let
let

Dolch & Fry Sight Words : Read Trace Write Handbook

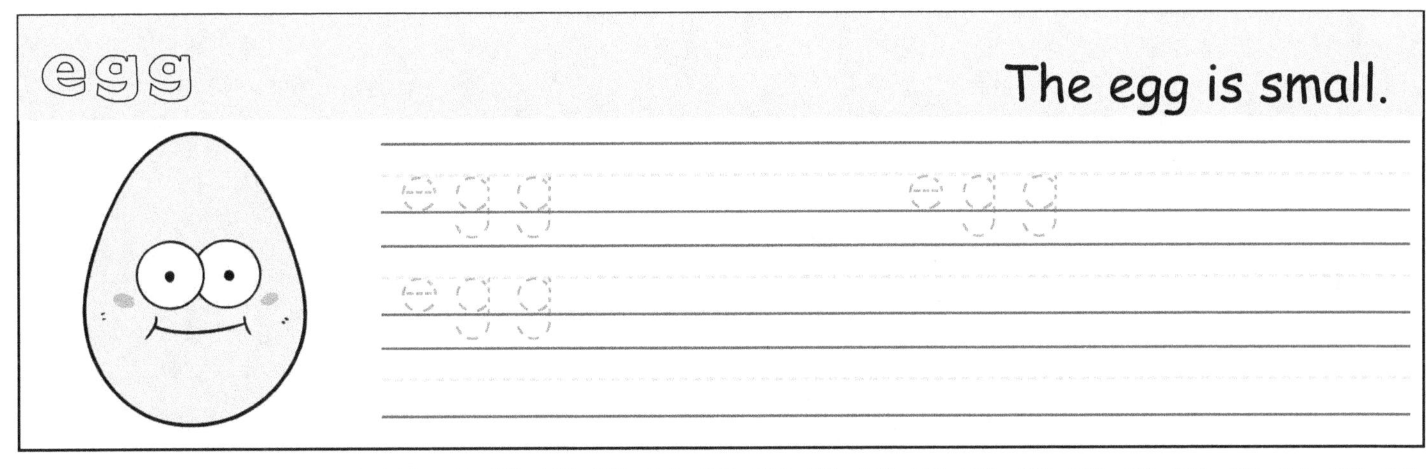

did

She did a great job.

did did
did

dog

The dog is adorable.

dog dog
dog

eat

The monkey will eat the banana.

eat eat
eat

egg

The egg is small.

egg egg
egg